Excel 2010:
Advanced
Student Manual

MOS Edition

Excel 2010: Advanced

Chief Executive Officer, Axzo Press:	Ken Wasnock
Series Designer and COO:	Adam A. Wilcox
Vice President, Operations:	Josh Pincus
Director of Publishing Systems Development:	Dan Quackenbush
Developmental Editor:	Laurie Perry
Copyeditor:	Catherine Oliver
Keytester:	Cliff Coryea

Trademarks

ILT Series is a trademark of Axzo Press.

Some of the product names and company names used in this book have been used for identification purposes only and may be trademarks or registered trademarks of their respective manufacturers and sellers.

Disclaimer

We reserve the right to revise this publication and make changes from time to time in its content without notice.

Student Manual
ISBN 10: 1-4260-2159-3
ISBN 13: 978-1-4260-2159-6

Printed in the United States of America
1 2 3 4 5 GL 06 05 04 03

Contents

Introduction

After reading this introduction, you will know how to:

A Use ILT Series manuals in general.

B Use prerequisites, a target student description, course objectives, and a skills inventory to properly set your expectations for the course.

C Re-key this course after class.

Topic A: About the manual

ILT Series philosophy

Our manuals facilitate your learning by providing structured interaction with the software itself. While we provide text to explain difficult concepts, the hands-on activities are the focus of our courses. By paying close attention as your instructor leads you through these activities, you will learn the skills and concepts effectively.

We believe strongly in the instructor-led class. During class, focus on your instructor. Our manuals are designed and written to facilitate your interaction with your instructor, and not to call attention to manuals themselves.

We believe in the basic approach of setting expectations, delivering instruction, and providing summary and review afterwards. For this reason, lessons begin with objectives and end with summaries. We also provide overall course objectives and a course summary to provide both an introduction to and closure on the entire course.

Manual components

The manuals contain these major components:

- Table of contents
- Introduction
- Units
- Course summary
- Glossary
- Index

Each element is described below.

Table of contents

The table of contents acts as a learning roadmap.

Introduction

The introduction contains information about our training philosophy and our manual components, features, and conventions. It contains target student, prerequisite, objective, and setup information for the specific course.

Units

Units are the largest structural component of the course content. A unit begins with a title page that lists objectives for each major subdivision, or topic, within the unit. Within each topic, conceptual and explanatory information alternates with hands-on activities. Units conclude with a summary comprising one paragraph for each topic, and an independent practice activity that gives you an opportunity to practice the skills you've learned.

The conceptual information takes the form of text paragraphs, exhibits, lists, and tables. The activities are structured in two columns, one telling you what to do, the other providing explanations, descriptions, and graphics.

Course summary

This section provides a text summary of the entire course. It is useful for providing closure at the end of the course. The course summary also indicates the next course in this series, if there is one, and lists additional resources you might find useful as you continue to learn about the software.

Glossary

The glossary provides definitions for all of the key terms used in this course.

Index

The index at the end of this manual makes it easy for you to find information about a particular software component, feature, or concept.

Manual conventions

We've tried to keep the number of elements and the types of formatting to a minimum in the manuals. This aids in clarity and makes the manuals more classically elegant looking. But there are some conventions and icons you should know about.

Item	Description
Italic text	In conceptual text, indicates a new term or feature.
Bold text	In unit summaries, indicates a key term or concept. In an independent practice activity, indicates an explicit item that you select, choose, or type.
`Code font`	Indicates code or syntax.

`Longer strings of ►`
`   code will look ►`
`   like this.`
	In the hands-on activities, any code that's too long to fit on a single line is divided into segments by one or more continuation characters (►). This code should be entered as a continuous string of text.

Select **bold item**	In the left column of hands-on activities, bold sans-serif text indicates an explicit item that you select, choose, or type.
Keycaps like ↵ ENTER	Indicate a key on the keyboard you must press.

Hands-on activities

The hands-on activities are the most important parts of our manuals. They are divided into two primary columns. The "Here's how" column gives short instructions to you about what to do. The "Here's why" column provides explanations, graphics, and clarifications. Here's a sample:

Do it!

A-1: Creating a commission formula

Here's how	Here's why
1 Open Sales	This is an oversimplified sales compensation worksheet. It shows sales totals, commissions, and incentives for five sales reps.
2 Observe the contents of cell F4	F4 ▼ = =E4*C_Rate
	The commission rate formulas use the name "C_Rate" instead of a value for the commission rate.

For these activities, we have provided a collection of data files designed to help you learn each skill in a real-world business context. As you work through the activities, you will modify and update these files. Of course, you might make a mistake and therefore want to re-key the activity starting from scratch. To make it easy to start over, you will rename each data file at the end of the first activity in which the file is modified. Our convention for renaming files is to add the word "My" to the beginning of the file name. In the above activity, for example, a file called "Sales" is being used for the first time. At the end of this activity, you would save the file as "My sales," thus leaving the "Sales" file unchanged. If you make a mistake, you can start over using the original "Sales" file.

In some activities, however, it might not be practical to rename the data file. If you want to retry one of these activities, ask your instructor for a fresh copy of the original data file.

Topic B: Setting your expectations

Properly setting your expectations is essential to your success. This topic will help you do that by providing:

- Prerequisites for this course
- A description of the target student
- A list of the objectives for the course
- A skills assessment for the course

Course prerequisites

Before taking this course, you should be familiar with personal computers and the use of a keyboard and a mouse. Furthermore, this course assumes that you've completed the following courses or have equivalent experience:

- *Windows 7: Basic*, *Windows Vista: Basic*, or *Windows XP: Basic*
- *Excel 2010: Basic*
- *Excel 2010: Intermediate*

Target student

Before taking this course, you should be comfortable using a personal computer and Microsoft Windows (preferably, Windows 7). You should have some experience with Excel 2010 and should be familiar with intermediate-level tasks, such as sorting data, linking worksheets, and outlining and consolidating data. You will get the most out of this course if your goal is to become proficient in performing advanced tasks, such as using logical, statistical, financial, and date functions, creating nested functions, working with data tables, exporting and importing data, performing what-if analyses, and recording macros.

Course objectives

These overall course objectives will give you an idea about what to expect from the course. It is also possible that they will help you see that this course is not the right one for you. If you think you either lack the prerequisite knowledge or already know most of the subject matter to be covered, you should let your instructor know that you think you are misplaced in the class.

Note: In addition to the general objectives listed below, specific Microsoft Office Specialist exam objectives are listed at the beginning of each topic (where applicable).

After completing this course, you will know how to:

- Use the IF and SUMIF functions to calculate a value based on specified criteria; use a nested IF function to evaluate complex conditions; and use the ROUND function to round off numbers;

- Use the PMT function to calculate periodic payments for a loan; use Date and Time functions to calculate duration in years, months, and days or time; display, print, and hide formulas; create array formulas to perform multiple calculations on multiple sets of data at one time; and change calculation options and iteration limits.

- Use the VLOOKUP and HLOOKUP functions to find values in worksheet data; use the MATCH function to find the relative position of a value in a range; use the INDEX function to find the value of a cell at a given position in a range; and use data tables to project values.

- Use the Data Validation feature to validate data entered in cells; and use database functions to summarize data values that meet criteria you specify.

- Export data from Excel to other formats, and import data from a text file into an Excel workbook; import XML data into a workbook, and export data from a workbook to an XML data file; and use Microsoft Query and the Web query feature to import data from external databases.

- Use the Goal Seek and Solver utilities to meet a target output for a formula by adjusting the values in the input cells; use the Analysis ToolPak to perform statistical analysis; and create scenarios to save various sets of input values that produce different results.

- Run a macro to perform tasks automatically; record macros; assign a macro to a command button and a button in the worksheet; use a button to run the macro; create an Auto_Open macro; edit a macro by editing VBA code; and create a custom function to perform calculations when built-in functions are not available.

Skills inventory

Use the following form to gauge your skill level entering the class. For each skill listed, rate your familiarity from 1 to 5, with five being the most familiar. *This is not a test.* Rather, it is intended to provide you with an idea of where you're starting from at the beginning of class. If you're wholly unfamiliar with all the skills, you might not be ready for the class. If you think you already understand all of the skills, you might need to move on to the next course in the series. In either case, you should let your instructor know as soon as possible.

Skill	1	2	3	4	5
Using logical functions (IF, OR, AND, and NOT)					
Using a formula to apply conditional formatting					
Using math and statistical functions (SUMIF, COUNTIF, AVERAGEIF, SUMIFS, COUNTIFS, AVERAGEIFS, and ROUND)					
Using the PMT function					
Using date functions (YEAR, DAYS360, and NETWORKDAYS)					
Calculating time					
Creating array formulas					
Using the VLOOKUP, MATCH, and INDEX functions					
Using data tables to project values					
Validating data					
Using database functions					
Importing and exporting text files					
Importing and exporting XML data					
Using Microsoft Query and Web query					
Using Goal Seek and Solver					
Using the Analysis ToolPak					
Creating scenarios					
Running and recording macros					
Assigning macros to command buttons					
Editing VBA modules					
Creating custom functions					

Topic C: Re-keying the course

If you have the proper hardware and software, you can re-key this course after class. This section explains what you'll need in order to do so, and how to do it.

Hardware requirements

Your personal computer should have:

- 1 GHz or faster 32- or 64-bit processor
- At least 1 GB of RAM
- 2 GB of hard-disk space after operating system install
- Video adapter card compatible with DirectX 9 or newer, with at least 64 MB video memory
- A keyboard and a mouse
- A monitor at 1024×768 resolution or higher
- Printer (useful but not required)
- DVD drive if you'll be installing via disc

Software requirements

You will also need the following software:

- Windows 7 (You can also use Windows XP or Windows Vista, but the screen shots in this course were taken in Windows 7, so your screens might look somewhat different.)
- Microsoft Office 2010
- A printer driver (An actual printer is not required, but you will not be able to get an exact preview in Print Preview without a printer driver installed.)

Network requirements

The following network components and connectivity are also required for re-keying this course:

- Internet access, for the following purposes:
  - Updating the Windows operating system and Microsoft Office 2010
  - Downloading the Student Data files from www.axzopress.com (if necessary)
  - Accessing the sample OLAP database in Activity C-3 of the unit titled "Exporting and importing."

Setup instructions to re-key the course

Before you re-key the course, you will need to perform the following steps.

1 Use Windows Update to install all available critical updates and service packs.

2 With a flat-panel display, we recommend using the panel's native resolution for best results. Color depth/quality should be set to High (24 bit) or higher.

Please note that your display settings or resolution may differ from the author's, so your screens might not exactly match the screen shots in this manual.

3 If necessary, reset any Excel 2010 defaults that you have changed. If you do not wish to reset the defaults, you can still re-key the course, but some activities might not work exactly as documented.

- In the Excel Options dialog box, reset the Quick Access Toolbar to its default state.

4 If you have the data disc that came with this manual, locate the Student Data folder on it and copy it to your Windows desktop.

If you don't have the data disc, you can download the Student Data files for the course:

a Connect to http://downloads.logicaloperations.com.

b Enter the course title or search by part to locate this course

c Click the course title to display a list of available downloads.
Note: Data Files are located under the Instructor Edition of the course.

d Click the link(s) for downloading the Student Data files.

e Create a folder named Student Data on the desktop of your computer.

f Double-click the downloaded zip file(s) and drag the contents into the Student Data folder.

U n i t 1

Logical and statistical functions

Complete this unit, and you'll know how to:

A Use logical functions to calculate values based on specified criteria, and use nested functions and the ROUND function.

B Use math and statistical functions to conditionally summarize, count, and average data.

Topic A: Logical functions

This topic covers the following Microsoft Office Specialist objectives for exam 77-882: Excel 2010.

#	Objective
5.4	**Apply conditional logic in a formula**
	5.4.1 Create a formula with values that match conditions
	5.4.2 Edit defined conditions in a formula
	5.4.3 Use a series of conditional logic values in a formula
8.3	**Apply conditional formatting**
	8.3.3 Use the IF function to apply conditional formatting

This topic covers the following Microsoft Office Specialist objectives for exam 77-888: Excel Expert 2010.

#	Objective
2.4	**Apply functions in formulas**
	2.4.1 Find and correct errors in functions

The IF function

Explanation

You can use conditional logic in a formula to return a specific result depending on whether a certain test, or condition, is met. If the condition is true, one result will be displayed. If the condition is false, a different result will be displayed. Microsoft Excel 2010 provides several logical functions you can use for conditionally evaluating a calculation: IF, AND, OR, NOT, and IFERROR.

The IF function evaluates a condition, or logical test. If the condition is true, the function returns a specific value. Otherwise, it returns another value. The syntax of the IF function is:

```
IF(logical_test,value_if_true,value_if_false)
```

In this syntax, `logical_test` is the criterion you want the function to evaluate, `value_if_true` is the value to be returned if the condition is true, and `value_if_false` is the value to be returned if the condition is false.

Editing conditions in a formula

The techniques used to edit formulas are the same as those used to edit other cell data. You can either:

- Click the formula bar to edit the formula.
- Double-click the cell and edit the formula in the cell.

When the formula is activated, the color of the cell references in the formula match the outline color in the worksheet. Also, the ScreenTip identifies the function component that is being edited. In Exhibit 1-1, for example, the insertion point is to the left of F8, so "logical_test" is bold.

	Salesperson	Sales per quarter				Total sales	Commission
		Qtr1	Qtr2	Qtr3	Qtr4		
3							
4	Sales goal:	$8,500					
5							
6	Salesperson	Sales per quarter				Total sales	Commission
7		Qtr1	Qtr2	Qtr3	Qtr4		
8	Bill MacArthur	$2,500	$2,750	$3,500	$3,700		=IF(F8>$B$4,F8*2%,"NA")
9	Jamie Morrison	$3,560	$3,000	$1,700	$2,000	$10,260	IF(logical_test, [value_if_true], [value_if_false])
10	Maureen O'Conno	$4,500	$4,000	$3,500	$3,700	$15,700	$314
11	Rebecca Austin	$3,250	$2,725	$3,000	$3,250	$12,225	$245
12	Paul Anderson	$2,520	$2,000	$2,500	$2,700	$9,720	$194

Exhibit 1-1: Editing a formula

Do it!

A-1:   Using the IF function

The files for this activity are in Student Data folder **Unit 1\Topic A**.

Here's how	Here's why
1 Start Excel	
Close the blank workbook	
2 Open Commission	This workbook contains four worksheets.
3 Save the workbook as **My commission**	In the current topic folder.
Verify that the If sheet is active	
4 Select G8	You'll use the IF function to calculate the commission for each salesperson. If the total-sales value is greater than the sales-goal value in cell B4, the commission should be calculated as 2% of the total sales. Otherwise, "Not applicable" should appear in the cell.
Type **=IF(F8>$B$4,**	In this function, "F8>$B$4" is the condition that will be evaluated. The reference to B4 is absolute (expressed as $B$4) because you'll AutoFill the cell to the ones below, and the other formulas should all refer to B4.
5 Type **F8*2%,**	"F8*2%" is the value to be returned if the condition is true.
Type **"NA")**	"NA" is the value to be returned if the condition is false.
6 Press ⏎ ENTER	The value NA appears in G8. Because the condition F8>B4 is false ($7,450<$8,500), the value NA is returned.

7 Copy the formula in G8 to G9:G22

(Use the AutoFill handle.) To calculate the remaining commissions.

Observe the Commission column

Commission
NA
$205
$314
$245
$194
NA
$337
$242
NA
$178
NA
$211
$286
$269
NA

You'll see the commission amount for each salesperson.

8 Double-click G8

To edit the formula directly in the cell. Notice that the B4 cell reference in the formula and the cell outline are the same green color. This color coding can be useful when you're editing complicated formulas.

Press (ESC)

To close Edit mode.

9 Update the workbook

Using a formula to apply conditional formatting

Explanation

Most of the options on the Conditional Formatting menu will be satisfactory for your needs. However, there might be situations when you want to use a formula to apply conditional formatting. You use the New Formatting Rule dialog box to enter a logical formula, and when the result is true, the specified formatting will be applied.

To do so, you can create a conditional formatting rule, as follows:

1 Select the range that the rule will be applied to.
2 In the Styles group, click Conditional Formatting and choose New Rule.
3 Under Select a Rule Type, select "Use a formula to determine which cells to format."
4 In the "Format values where this formula is true" box, enter the formula.
5 Click Format and use the Number, Font, Border, and Fill tabs to specify the formatting.
6 Click OK twice.

Do it!

A-2: Using a formula to apply conditional formatting

Here's how	Here's why
1 Select B8:E22	Notice that the status bar displays the average, count, and sum of the selected range. The average is $2,748. You'll create a formula that applies a yellow fill to the cells whose values are lower than the average.
2 On the Home tab, in the Styles group, click **Conditional Formatting**	
3 Choose **New Rule...**	
Under Select a Rule Type, select **Use a formula to determine which cells to format**	Select a Rule Type: ▶ Format all cells based on their values ▶ Format only cells that contain ▶ Format only top or bottom ranked values ▶ Format only values that are above or below average ▶ Format only unique or duplicate values ▶ Use a formula to determine which cells to format
4 In the "Format values where this formula is true" box, enter **=B8<AVERAGE(**	
In the worksheet, select B8:E22	The New Formatting Rule dialog box collapses so you can select the worksheet cells. The selected range is added with absolute references.
Type **)**	**Format values where this formula is true:** =B8<AVERAGE($B$8:$E$22) To complete the formula with a closing parenthesis.

5 Click **Format**	To open the Format Cells dialog box.
Click the **Fill** tab and select a yellow fill color	
Click **OK**	To close the Format Cells dialog box.
6 Click **OK**	To save and apply the new rule.
7 Deselect the range	

Qtr1	Qtr2	Qtr3	Qtr4
$2,500	$2,750	$3,500	$3,700
$3,560	$3,000	$1,700	$2,000
$4,500	$4,000	$3,500	$3,700
$3,250	$2,725	$3,000	$3,250
$2,520	$2,000	$2,500	$2,700
$1,500	$1,700	$1,800	$2,000
$4,590	$4,050	$4,500	$3,700
$3,660	$3,200	$3,000	$2,250
$1,790	$1,800	$2,000	$2,200
$1,700	$1,950	$2,500	$2,750
$1,650	$2,000	$1,500	$1,750
$2,050	$2,500	$2,800	$3,200
$3,425	$3,750	$4,000	$3,120
$4,540	$2,700	$3,000	$3,200
$1,200	$1,700	$1,800	$2,000

All values less than the average are colored yellow.

Update the workbook

Creating nested functions

Explanation

You can use nested functions to perform more complex calculations. A *nested function* is contained within another function and serves as an argument of that function. For example, an IF function can contain other IF functions as arguments. It can also contain the OR, AND, or NOT functions.

The OR, AND, and NOT functions

In addition to IF, you can use the OR, AND, and NOT functions to conditionally evaluate a formula. While you can use OR, AND, and NOT by themselves, they are more helpful if used within an IF function. You can use the OR, AND, and NOT functions in an IF function to determine whether multiple conditions are true, whether some conditions are true, or whether a condition is *not* true. The syntax for these functions, when nested within an IF function, is described below.

With the OR function, only *one* of the conditions named needs to be true for the specified result to be displayed. Here's the syntax:

```
IF(OR(logical1,logical2),value_if true,value_if_false)
```

In the AND function, *all* conditions specified must be met for the `value_if_true` result to be returned.

```
IF(AND(logical1,logical2),value_if_true,value_if_false)
```

The NOT function reverses the value of its argument. In other words, you state the result you want if the condition specified is not true.

```
IF(NOT(logical),value_if true,value_if_false)
```

Sales goal:	$8,500									
Salesperson	**Sales per quarter**				**Total sales**	**Commission**	**Training completed**	**Year-end bonus**	**Winner's Circle**	**Further training**
	Qtr1	**Qtr2**	**Qtr3**	**Qtr4**						
Bill MacArthur	$1,500	$1,750	$1,500	$2,700	$7,450	NA	No	No bonus		Recommended
Jamie Morrison	$3,560	$3,000	$1,700	$2,000	$10,260	$205	No	No bonus		
Maureen O'Connor	$4,500	$4,000	$3,500	$3,700	$15,700	$314	No	No bonus		
Rebecca Austin	$3,250	$2,725	$3,000	$3,250	$12,225	$245	Yes	$183	Yes	
Paul Anderson	$2,520	$2,000	$2,500	$2,700	$9,720	$194	Yes	$146		
Cynthia Roberts	$1,500	$1,700	$1,800	$2,000	$7,000	NA	Yes	No bonus		Recommended
Rita Greg	$4,590	$4,050	$4,500	$3,700	$16,840	$337	No	No bonus		
Trevor Johnson	$3,660	$3,200	$3,000	$2,250	$12,110	$242	Yes	$182	Yes	
Kevin Meyers	$1,790	$1,800	$2,000	$2,200	$7,790	NA	Yes	No bonus		Recommended
Adam Long	$1,700	$1,950	$2,500	$2,750	$8,900	$178	No	No bonus		
Kendra James	$1,650	$2,000	$1,500	$1,750	$6,900	NA	No	No bonus		Recommended
Michael Lee	$2,050	$2,500	$2,800	$3,200	$10,550	$211	Yes	$158		
Sandra Lawrence	$3,425	$3,750	$4,000	$3,120	$14,295	$286	Yes	$214	Yes	
Mary Smith	$4,540	$2,700	$3,000	$3,200	$13,440	$269	No	No bonus		
Annie Philips	$1,200	$1,700	$1,800	$2,000	$6,700	NA	Yes	No bonus		Recommended

Exhibit 1-2: A portion of the worksheet showing the results of function calculations

Do it!   **A-3: Using OR, AND, and NOT as nested functions**

Here's how	Here's why
1 Click the NOT, AND, OR sheet	You'll nest these functions within IF functions to create more complex calculations.
2 In I8, enter **=IF(OR**	To enter the first part of the nested OR function. You'll use this function to determine whether an employee receives a year-end bonus.
Type **(G8="NA",H8="No"),**	To enter the logical tests you will use to perform the calculation.
3 Type **"No bonus",F8*1.5%)**	

f_x `=IF(OR(G8="NA",H8="No"),"No bonus",F8*1.5%)`

	To enter the values that will be returned if either condition is true. The complete formula should look like the one shown above.
4 Press ⏎ ENTER	To complete the formula and calculate the result. "No bonus" appears in cell I8.
Copy the formula to I9:I22	
Observe the Year-end bonus column	As shown in Exhibit 1-2, many employees do not get a bonus because they did not meet or exceed the sales goal or they did not complete training. Remember that only one of the conditions in the OR function needs to be true in order for the function to return the first specified value, which is "No bonus."
5 Select J8	You'll create a nested AND function to determine which employees belong in the Winner's Circle.
6 Enter the formula shown:	

f_x `=IF(AND(H8="Yes",F8>12000),"Yes","")`

	In this formula, both logical tests (conditions) must be true in order to return the first value of "Yes." An employee must have completed training *and* exceeded $12,000 in total sales in order to be in the Winner's Circle.
7 Copy the formula to J9:J22	Only three employees meet both conditions outlined in the formula: Rebecca Austin, Trevor Johnson, and Sandra Lawrence.

8	Select K8	You'll use a nested NOT function to determine which employees should get more training.
9	Enter the formula shown:	

> *fx*   =IF(NOT(F8>=$B$4),"Recommended","")

In this formula, if the condition specified (F8>=$B$4) is *not* true, the value "Recommended" will be returned; otherwise, the empty string value "" (or blank) will be returned.

10	Copy the formula to K9:K22	Five employees did not make the sales goal of $8,500, so further training is recommended. Your worksheet should look like Exhibit 1-2.

    Update the workbook

Nested IF functions

Explanation

You use nested IF functions to evaluate multiple conditions. For example, use a second IF function as the `value_if_false` argument of the first IF function.

Do it!

A-4: Using nested IF functions

Here's how	Here's why
1 Click the Nested If sheet	
Observe the text box in the worksheet	Sales Commission Below 5000 None Between 5000-15000 1% Between 15000-25000 1.5% Above 25000 2%
	This sheet calculates commissions based on the range in which each employee's sales fall.
2 Select C7	You'll calculate commissions based on the total sales and the various commission rates.
Type **=IF(B7>25000, B7*2%,**	The first IF function is applied when the total-sales value in B7 is greater than 25,000. If this condition is true, the commission is calculated as 2% of the total sales.
Type **IF(B7>15000, B7*1.5%,**	If the first condition (B7>25000) is false, this condition (B7>15000) is evaluated. If it is true, the commission is calculated as 1.5% of the total sales.
3 Type **IF(B7>5000, B7*1%, 0)))**	The complete formula should look like the screen shot shown below.

f_x | =IF(B7>25000,B7*2%,IF(B7>15000,B7*1.5%,IF(B7>5000,B7*1%,0)))

	If both the first condition (B7>25000) and the second condition (B7>15000) are false, this third condition (B7>5000) is evaluated. If this condition is true, the commission is calculated as 1% of total sales. If this final condition is false, 0 (zero) is returned.
Press (← ENTER)	Because B7 (12,450) is greater than 5000 but less than 15,000, a 1% commission is calculated, and the value $124.50 appears in C7.
4 Copy the formula in C7 to C8:C21	To calculate the remaining commissions.
5 Update the workbook	

The IFERROR function

Explanation

You can use the IFERROR function to check a formula for errors and to replace Excel's default error message with a message you specify. For example, if you try to divide a number by zero in a formula, the error message #DIV/0! appears in the cell by default. You can replace this message with your own by using IFERROR.

The syntax for the IFERROR function is:

```
IFERROR(value,value_if_error)
```

where `value` is the argument you want to check for an error, and `value_if_error` is the message you want to display if an error is found. If no error is found in the formula, the result of the formula is displayed.

Do it!

A-5:   Using the IFERROR function

Here's how	Here's why
1 Click the IFERROR sheet	You'll use the IFERROR function to find calculation errors and identify them with your own error message.
2 Select D7	
Type **=IFERROR(**	To begin the IFERROR function.
Type **B7/C7,**	To enter the value you want the function to calculate and check for errors.
3 Type **"Check price")**	To specify the error message to be displayed if the function finds an error.
Press (↵ ENTER)	To complete the formula and calculate a result for D7.
4 Copy the formula in D7 to D8:D19	The error message "Check price" appears in D8 and D17 because the formula tried to divide a number by zero.
5 Update and close the workbook	

Topic B: Math and statistical functions

This topic covers the following Microsoft Office Specialist objectives for exam 77-888: Excel Expert 2010.

#	Objective
2.3	**Perform data summary tasks**
	2.3.2 Use a SUMIFS function
2.4	**Apply functions in formulas**
	2.4.3 Use statistical functions

The SUMIF function

Explanation

You can conditionally summarize, count, and average data by using math and statistical functions. These functions include SUMIF, COUNTIF, AVERAGEIF, SUMIFS, COUNTIFS, and AVERAGEIFS.

You use the SUMIF function when you want to add values within a range of cells based on the evaluation of a criterion in another range. The syntax of the SUMIF function is:

```
SUMIF(range,criteria,sum_range)
```

In this syntax, `range` is the range in which the function will test the criterion specified in `criteria`. The argument `sum_range` specifies the actual cells whose values are to be added. `Sum_range` is optional; if it's omitted, the cells specified in `range` are evaluated by `criteria`, and they are added if they match `criteria`.

Do it!

B-1: Using SUMIF

The files for this activity are in Student Data folder **Unit 1\Topic B**.

Here's how	Here's why
1 Open Sales	
Save the workbook as **My sales**	In the current topic folder.
2 Click the SumIf sheet	
3 Select B29	You'll sum up the sales for the East region for the prior year.
Type **=SUMIF(Region,**	In the formula, "Region" is the named range of cells B8:B22, which SUMIF will evaluate.
Type **"East",**	"East" is the evaluation criterion. You must include quotes around this value because it is a label.

4 Type **Sales_prior)**

  Press (↵ ENTER)

5 In B30, display the East region's total sales for the current year

6 In E29, display the North region's total sales for the prior year

7 In E30, display the North region's total sales for the current year

8 Fill in the current and prior years' sales information for the South and West regions

"Sales_prior" is the range C8:C22, which will be summed based on the criterion.

The value of the East region's total sales for the prior year, $43,685.00, appears in B29.

(Use the name of the range D8:D22, Sales_current, in the SUMIF function.) The value $56,320.00 appears.

(Specify North as the evaluation criterion.) The value $65,040.00 appears.

The value $70,950.00 appears.

East			North	
Total sales-prior year	$43,685.00		Total sales-prior year	$65,040.00
Total sales-current year	$56,320.00		Total sales-current year	$70,950.00
Current year average			Current year average	
Increase above target			Increase above target	
Stores over target			Stores over target	
Average increase			Average increase	

South			West	
Total sales-prior year	$35,465.00		Total sales-prior year	$28,600.00
Total sales-current year	$44,680.00		Total sales-current year	$39,980.00
Current year average			Current year average	
Increase above target			Increase above target	
Stores over target			Stores over target	
Average increase			Average increase	

9 Update the workbook

The COUNTIF function

Explanation

You use the COUNTIF function to count the number of cells in a range that meet your specified criteria.

The syntax for the COUNTIF function is:

```
COUNTIF(range,criteria)
```

`Range` is the cell or range of cells to count that meet the stated criterion. Text values and blank cells are ignored. `Criteria` can be text, numbers, expressions, or cell references that identify the cells to be counted.

Do it!

B-2: Using COUNTIF

Here's how	Here's why
1 Select G8	**# Stores meeting current goals:**
	You'll count the number of stores that have met or exceeded the current year's sales goal of $15,000.
2 Type **=COUNTIF(**	To start the function.
Type **Sales_current,**	To designate the range in which you will count the cells that meet your criterion.
Type **">=15000")**	To specify the criterion to be met.
3 Press ⏎ ENTER	**# Stores meeting current goals:** 9
	To complete the function and return the result. The value 9 appears in the cell because there are nine stores meeting or exceeding the sales goal.
4 Update the workbook	

The AVERAGEIF function

Explanation

AVERAGEIF, like SUMIF and COUNTIF, is a conditional math function. Use AVERAGEIF to conditionally average a range of numbers.

The syntax for the AVERAGEIF function is:

```
AVERAGEIF(range,criteria,average_range)
```

`Range` is the cell or range of cells you want to average, and `criteria` is the number, expression, cell reference, or text that identifies which cells should be averaged. `Average_range` is the corresponding set of cells you want to average. If you omit this, `range` will be used instead.

Summary			
East		**North**	
Total sales-prior year	$43,685.00	Total sales-prior year	$65,040.00
Total sales-current year	$56,320.00	Total sales-current year	$70,950.00
Current year average	$14,080.00	Current year average	$17,737.50
Increase above target		Increase above target	
Stores over target		Stores over target	
Average increase		Average increase	
South		**West**	
Total sales-prior year	$35,465.00	Total sales-prior year	$28,600.00
Total sales-current year	$44,680.00	Total sales-current year	$39,980.00
Current year average	$11,170.00	Current year average	$13,326.67
Increase above target		Increase above target	
Stores over target		Stores over target	
Average increase		Average increase	

Exhibit 1-3: The Summary section on the SumIF sheet

Do it!

B-3: Using AVERAGEIF

Here's how	Here's why
1 Select B31	You'll calculate the average of current-year sales for the East region.
2 Type **=AVERAGEIF(**	To begin the function.
Type **Region,"East",**	To designate Region as the range, and East as the criterion for that range.
Type **Sales_current)**	To designate the current year's sales in column D as the range from which the actual cells to be averaged will be drawn.
3 Press ⏎ ENTER	To finish the function and calculate the result. Cell B31displays $14,080.00, which is the average of current-year sales for the East region.
4 Calculate the average of current-year sales for the remaining regions	Compare your screen to Exhibit 1-3.
5 Update the workbook	

SUMIFS, COUNTIFS, and AVERAGEIFS

Explanation

Although SUMIF, COUNTIF, and AVERAGEIF are useful for conditionally summarizing data, they allow only one criterion. To remedy this limitation, Excel 2010 provides the SUMIFS, COUNTIFS, and AVERAGEIFS functions, which enable you to easily sum, count, and average values in a range while using multiple criteria.

SUMIFS

The syntax for the SUMIFS function is:

    SUMIFS(sum_range,criteria_range1,criteria1,criteria_range2,
    criteria2)

Sum_range is the cell or range you want to sum. Criteria_range1 and criteria_range2 are the ranges in which the function evaluates the related criteria; criteria1 and criteria2 are the actual criteria. Note that in the SUMIFS function, the sum_range argument appears first (rather than last, as in SUMIF).

COUNTIFS

The syntax for the COUNTIFS function is:

    COUNTIFS(range1,criteria1,range2,criteria2)

Range1 and range2 are the ranges where the related criteria are evaluated. Criteria1 and criteria2 are the criteria by which the cells or ranges are evaluated.

AVERAGEIFS

The syntax for the AVERAGEIFS function is:

    AVERAGEIFS(average_range,criteria_range1,criteria1,
    criteria_range2,criteria2)

Average_range is the range of cells you want to average. Criteria_range1 and criteria_range2 are the ranges where the function evaluates the related criteria. Criteria1 and criteria2 are the criteria by which the specified cells will be evaluated.

Summary				
East			**North**	
Total sales-prior year	$43,685.00		Total sales-prior year	$65,040.00
Total sales-current year	$56,320.00		Total sales-current year	$70,950.00
Current year average	$14,080.00		Current year average	$17,737.50
Increase above target	$6,985.00		Increase above target	$3,660.00
Stores over target	2		Stores over target	3
Average increase	$3,492.50		Average increase	$1,220.00
South			**West**	
Total sales-prior year	$35,465.00		Total sales-prior year	$28,600.00
Total sales-current year	$44,680.00		Total sales-current year	$39,980.00
Current year average	$11,170.00		Current year average	$13,326.67
Increase above target	$7,105.00		Increase above target	$5,630.00
Stores over target	2		Stores over target	1
Average increase	$3,552.50		Average increase	$5,630.00

Exhibit 1-4: The completed Summary section of the SumIF sheet

B-4: Using SUMIFS, COUNTIFS, and AVERAGEIFS

Here's how	Here's why
1 Select B32	You'll use the SUMIFS function to sum the increase in sales over the target goal for stores in the East region.
2 Type **=SUMIFS(**	To begin the function.
Type **E8:E22,**	To specify the range containing the cells to be summarized. You want to use the amount of increase or decrease in sales.
Type **Region,"East",**	To specify the East region as the first criteria range and the first criterion by which to evaluate the range.
Type **Sales_current,">15000")**	To specify the second criteria range and the second criterion. The formula will check to see if the current sales number is larger than the target of $15,000.
3 Press ⏎ ENTER	To enter the function. The value $6,985.00 is displayed. This is the total of the increase in sales over the target goal for all stores in the East region.
4 Calculate the increase in sales above the target goal for the remaining regions	

East				North	
Total sales-prior year	$43,685.00			Total sales-prior year	$65,040.00
Total sales-current year	$56,320.00			Total sales-current year	$70,950.00
Current year average	$14,080.00			Current year average	$17,737.50
Increase above target	$6,985.00			Increase above target	$3,660.00
Stores over target				Stores over target	
Average increase				Average increase	

South				West	
Total sales-prior year	$35,465.00			Total sales-prior year	$28,600.00
Total sales-current year	$44,680.00			Total sales-current year	$39,980.00
Current year average	$11,170.00			Current year average	$13,326.67
Increase above target	$7,105.00			Increase above target	$5,630.00
Stores over target				Stores over target	
Average increase				Average increase	

5 Select B33	You'll calculate the number of stores in the East region that exceeded the target sales goal.
Type **=COUNTIFS(**	To begin the function.

6	Type **Region,"East",**	To specify the first range and the criterion by which the range will be evaluated.
	Type **Sales_current,">15000")**	To specify the second range and the criterion by which it will be evaluated.
7	Press (↵ ENTER)	To complete the function and display the result. Two stores in the East region exceeded the sales target of $15,000.
	Calculate the number of stores exceeding the target sales goal in each of the remaining regions	Compare your Summary section to Exhibit 1-4.
8	Select B34	You'll use the AVERAGEIFS function to calculate the average increase in sales for those stores exceeding the target goal.
9	Type **=AVERAGEIFS(**	To begin the function.
	Type **E8:E22,**	To specify the range containing the cells to be averaged.
	Type **Region,"East",**	To specify the first criteria range and the first criterion.
10	Type **Sales_current,">15000")**	To specify the second criteria range and the second criterion.
	Press (↵ ENTER)	To complete the function and display the result; $3,492.50 appears in B34.
11	Calculate the average increase in sales for the remaining regions	Compare your Summary section to Exhibit 1-4.
	Update the workbook	

The ROUND function

Explanation

You can round off a value to a specified number of digits by using the ROUND function. The syntax of the ROUND function is:

```
ROUND(value,num_digits)
```

The first argument of the function is the value you want to round off. The second argument is the number of digits to which you want to round off that value. If num_digits is positive, the function rounds off the number to the specified number of decimal places. If num_digits is negative, the function rounds off the value to the left of the decimal point. For example, ROUND(126.87,1) returns 126.9, and ROUND(126.87,-1) returns 130.

Evaluation order of conditions

You might want to view the evaluation order of the conditions in a function to understand that function. To view the evaluation order:

1 Select the cell containing the function you want to evaluate. You can evaluate only one cell at a time.

2 On the Formulas tab, in the Formula Auditing group, click the Evaluate Formula button to open the Evaluate Formula dialog box, shown in Exhibit 1-5.

3 Click Step In to view the value in the selected cell.

4 Click Step Out to return to the function.

5 Click Evaluate to evaluate the underlined part of the function.

6 Click Close.

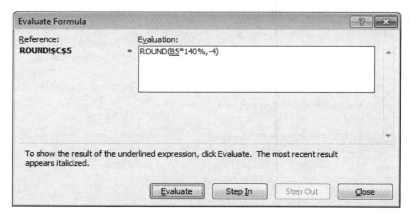

Exhibit 1-5: The Evaluate Formula dialog box

Do it! **B-5: Using ROUND**

Here's how	Here's why
1 Click the Round sheet	
2 Select C5	You'll calculate the target sales for Atlanta.
Enter **=B5*140%**	The target sales figure for the current year is calculated as 140% of the total sales for the prior year. The value $9,778,688.92 appears. You'll round the value in C5.
3 Edit C5 to read **=ROUND(B5*140%,-4)**	In this formula, "B5*140%" is the value to be rounded, and "-4" specifies that four digits to the left of the decimal point should be rounded. (The value should be rounded to the ten-thousands place.)
Press (↵ ENTER)	The value $9,780,000.00 is displayed.
4 Fill the formula down to C18	(Drag the Fill handle from C5 to C18.) To round off the target sales values for the remaining cities.
5 Select C5	You'll determine the order in which the ROUND function's components are evaluated.
6 Click the **Formulas** tab	
7 In the Formula Auditing group, click **Evaluate Formula**	To open the Evaluate Formula dialog box, shown in Exhibit 1-5. The ROUND function appears in the Evaluation box. In the function, B5 is underlined, indicating that the value in this cell is used to evaluate the function.
8 Click **Step In**	Reference: Evaluation: ROUND!$C$5 = ROUND(B5*140%,-4) └ **ROUND!$B$5** = *$6,984,777.80* To view the current value in B5, which is $6,984,777.80.
9 Click **Step Out**	Reference: Evaluation: **ROUND!$C$5** = ROUND(*6984777.8**<u>140%</u>,-4) To return to the formula. In the formula, B5 has been replaced by its current value. Notice that 140% is underlined, indicating that it will be evaluated next.

10 Click **Evaluate**	Reference: Evaluation: **ROUND!$C$5** = ROUND(6984777.8*1.4,-4)
	In the formula, 1.4 replaces 140%. The first argument of the ROUND function is underlined, indicating that it will be evaluated next.
Click **Evaluate**	Reference: Evaluation: **ROUND!$C$5** = ROUND(9778688.92,-4)
	The result of evaluation, 9778688.92, appears. The entire ROUND function is underlined. This indicates that the value 9778688.92 will be rounded off next.
Click **Evaluate**	Reference: Evaluation: **ROUND!$C$5** = $9,780,000.00
	The value $9,780,000.00 appears.
11 Click **Close**	To close the Evaluate Formula dialog box.
12 Update and close the workbook	

Unit summary: Logical and statistical functions

Topic A   In this topic, you used the **logical functions** IF, AND, OR, and NOT to evaluate a condition and return a value based on whether that condition is true or false. You also used **nested functions** to perform complex calculations. You learned that a nested IF function can be used to evaluate multiple conditions. Finally, you used the IFERROR function.

Topic B   In this topic, you used the **math and statistical functions** SUMIF, SUMIFS, COUNTIF, COUNTIFS, AVERAGEIF, and AVERAGEIFS to conditionally summarize, count, and average data. You also learned how to round off a number by using the ROUND function. Next, you learned how to view the **evaluation order** of the conditions in a function by using the Evaluate Formula dialog box.

Independent practice activity

In this activity, you'll enter calculations, such as a nested IF function.

The files for this activity are in Student Data folder **Unit 1\Unit summary**.

1 Open Performance.

2 Save the workbook as **My performance**.

3 Use a nested IF function to determine the performance grade for each salesperson based on the percentage of increase in sales. For example, if sales increased by more than 25%, the grade will be A, and so on. The criteria for all performance grades are given in the following table. (*Hint:* Scroll down to cell A100 to see the correct formula.)

Increase	Grade
Above 25%	A
15%–25%	B
0%–15%	C
Below 0%	D

4 Compare your Performance worksheet to Exhibit 1-6.

5 Update and close the workbook.

Outlander Spices					
Performance analysis					
Name	Prior year	Current year	Increase in sales	% Increase in sales	Performance grade
Malcolm Pingault	$3,922.76	$6,003.24	$2,080.48	34.66%	A
Shannon Lee	$4,290.58	$6,171.80	$1,881.22	30.48%	A
Melinda McGregor	$2,208.36	$2,859.73	$651.37	22.78%	B
James Overmire	$9,813.67	$9,000.33	($813.34)	-9.04%	D
Roger Williams	$2,147.21	$2,077.38	($69.83)	-3.36%	D
Annie Philips	$2,342.94	$2,775.05	$432.11	15.57%	B
Melissa James	$2,752.29	$2,597.66	($154.63)	-5.95%	D
Mary Smith	$8,280.28	$9,365.62	$1,085.34	11.59%	C
Rita Greg	$6,323.81	$8,376.45	$2,052.64	24.50%	B
Trevor Johnson	$9,916.93	$12,146.15	$2,229.22	18.35%	B
Paul Anderson	$5,600.02	$5,156.95	($443.07)	-8.59%	D
Rebecca Austin	$5,751.30	$6,969.75	$1,218.45	17.48%	B
Cynthia Roberts	$9,468.86	$10,504.12	$1,035.26	9.86%	C
Michael Lee	$6,453.70	$7,459.16	$1,005.46	13.48%	C
Sandra Lawrence	$4,480.39	$5,408.33	$927.94	17.16%	B
Kendra James	$9,283.00	$9,157.70	($125.30)	-1.37%	D
Total	$93,036.10	$106,029.41	$12,993.31	13.97%	

Exhibit 1-6: The Performance sheet after Step 3

Review questions

1 What is the syntax of the IF function?

2 What is a nested function?

3 If you want to view the evaluation order of a complex function, you can use the Evaluate Formula dialog box. How do you open this dialog box?

Unit 2

Financial and date functions

Complete this unit, and you'll know how to:

A Use the PMT function to calculate periodic payments for a loan.

B Use date and time functions to calculate duration, expressed as the number of days and hours.

C Use array formulas to perform multiple calculations on multiple sets of values.

D Display and print formulas.

Topic A: Financial functions

This topic covers the following Microsoft Office Specialist objectives for exam 77-888: Excel Expert 2010.

#	Objective
2.4	**Apply functions in formulas**
	2.4.6 Use financial functions

The PMT function

Explanation

Excel provides several financial functions for calculating such values as depreciation, future or present loan values, and loan payments. One financial function is the PMT function, which you can use to calculate loan payments.

The PMT function returns the periodic payments for a loan. The return value is negative if the amount is to be paid, and positive if the amount is to be obtained.

The syntax of the PMT function is:

    PMT(rate,nper,pv,fv,type)

The following table describes each argument of the PMT function:

Argument	Description
rate	The interest rate per period. For example, if you get a loan at 10% annual interest and you make monthly payments, the first argument will be 10%/12.
nper	The number of payments that have to be made to repay the loan. For example, if you have four years to pay back the loan, and you make monthly payments, the second argument will be 48 (4*12).
pv	The present value or the principal amount of the loan. This argument can also have a negative value. For example, if you give a loan of $12,000, the present value will be -12000. However, if you take a loan of $12,000, the present value will be 12000.
fv	(Optional) The future value of the loan—that is, its value after the last payment is made. If you omit the future value, it's assumed to be zero.
type	(Optional) Indicates when payments are due. This argument can have either of two values: 0 if payments are due at the end of the period, or 1 if payments are due at the beginning of the period. If you omit this argument, it's assumed to be zero.

Do it!

A-1:   Using the PMT function

The files for this activity are in Student Data folder **Unit 2\Topic A**.

Here's how	Here's why
1 Open Loan	
Save the workbook as **My loan**	In the current topic folder.
2 Click the PMT sheet	If necessary.
3 Select E6	You'll calculate the monthly payment to be made to AmericaBank.
Type **=PMT(D6%/12,**	In this formula, "D6%/12" is the monthly rate of interest.
Type **C6,B6)**	=PMT(D6%/12,C6,B6)
	"C6" refers to the cell containing the period of repayment, and "B6" refers to the cell containing the present value of the loan.
Press ⏎ ENTER	The value -$3,417.76 appears in E6. The negative sign signifies that you have to pay this amount.
4 Copy the formula in E6 to E7:E8 and E10:E11	To calculate the monthly payments for the remaining banks.
5 Change the value in C6 to **24**	When the number of payments goes down, the monthly payment amount increases.
6 Update and close the workbook	

Topic B: Date and time functions

This topic covers the following Microsoft Office Specialist objectives for exam 77-888: Excel Expert 2010.

#	Objective
2.4	**Apply functions in formulas**
	2.4.4 Use date functions
	2.4.5 Use time functions

Using date functions

Explanation

In Excel, dates are stored as sequential serial numbers. The serial number 1 is assigned to January 1, 1900. In this method, January 1, 2010 is serial number 40179. When a date is entered into a cell formatted as General, Excel automatically applies the Date format. For calculation purposes, the underlying value in the cell remains the serial number. To display the serial number in the cell, change the cell format to General or Number.

Excel provides a wide variety of built-in date functions that you can use to insert the current date in a cell or to calculate the number of days between the starting and ending dates. To insert a date function, click the Date & Time button in the Function Library group on the Formulas tab, and select the desired function. You can also click the Insert Function button to open the Insert Function dialog box.

TODAY

You use the TODAY function to enter the current date in the selected cell. The syntax is:

```
=TODAY()
```

YEAR

Use the YEAR function to return the year in the specified date serial number. Apply the General or Number format to the resulting value. The syntax for the YEAR function is:

```
=YEAR(serial_number)
```

You can also use this function to calculate the number of years between two dates. The formula would be:

```
=YEAR(serial_number)-YEAR(serial_number)
```

DAYS360

To calculate the number of days between a start date and an end date, use the DAYS360 function. This function is based on a 360-day year. The syntax for the DAYS360 function is:

```
=DAYS360(start_date,end_date)
```

To calculate the number of years between two dates, you can divide by 365 to get a more accurate result in years. If the resulting value is not a full year, then format the cell as Number to display the exact number of years with a decimal point. The syntax using the DAYS360 function would be:

```
=DAYS360(start_date,end_date)/365
```

NETWORKDAYS

You can use the NETWORKDAYS function to calculate the number of work days between the start date and the end date, excluding weekends. The Holidays argument is optional. The syntax is:

```
=NETWORKDAYS(start_date, end_date, [holidays])
```

Arguments in date functions

When entering arguments in the date functions, you can enter the date as *mm/dd/yyyy* and Excel will convert it to the serial number. If the date already appears in a cell, use the cell reference as the argument in the function.

Do it!

B-1:   Using date functions

The files for this activity are in Student Data folder **Unit 2\Topic B**.

Here's how	Here's why
1 Open HR dates	
Save the workbook as **My HR dates**	
Click the **Years of service** tab	If necessary.
2 Select E2	
Enter **=TODAY( )**	The current date appears in Date format.
3 In E5, enter **=YEAR($E$2)-YEAR(D5)**	*fx* =YEAR($E$2)-YEAR(D5) To calculate the number of years Davis Lee has been an employee. The answer looks odd because of the Date format.
Apply the **General** format to E5	The result is 12 years.
4 Calculate the remaining employees' years of service	

Hire date	Years of service
1/20/1998	12
9/15/2010	0
2/2/2009	1
3/1/2009	1
4/8/1995	15
6/7/2009	1
10/6/2008	2

Drag the fill handle down from E5 to E32. For employees who were hired this year, the years of service will be 0.

Here's how	Here's why
5 Update the workbook	
6 In F5, enter **=DAYS360(D5,$E$2)/365**	The DAYS360 function calculates the number of days between the hire date and the current date, based on a 360-day year. To find the number of years, you'll divide by 365. The result is formatted as a number with two decimal places.
7 Fill the formula down to E32	

Hire date	Years of service	
1/20/1998	12	12.58
9/15/2010	0	0.10
2/2/2009	1	1.69
3/1/2009	1	1.61
4/8/1995	15	15.32
6/7/2009	1	1.35
10/6/2008	2	2.01

Employees who were hired this year now show years of service as a decimal number (0.10).

8 Update the workbook

9 Click the **Training phases** tab | This worksheet contains dates for training that will occur in three phases. You want to calculate the number of workdays being spent on training.

10 In D5, enter
    =NETWORKDAYS(B5,C5)

| ✕ ✔ *fx* | =NETWORKDAYS(B5,C5) |

To calculate the number of actual workdays this time includes. The weekend days have been removed and the resulting number of days is 52.

Copy the formula to Phase II and Phase III

# of workdays
52
50
65

11 Observe G4:G12

Company holidays
1/1/2010
3/17/2010
4/20/2010
7/4/2010
9/3/2010
10/31/2010
11/25/2010
12/25/2010

This range contains the fictional company holidays for the year.

In E5, enter
=NETWORKDAYS(B5,C5,

You'll use the NETWORKDAYS function to calculate the number of workdays, excluding weekends and holidays.

Select G5:G12 and press F4

| ✕ ✔ *fx* | =NETWORKDAYS(B5,C5,$G$5:$G$12) |

To add the holiday argument as an absolute reference.

Press ↵ ENTER

The number of days was reduced by 1 because the 1/1/2010 holiday fell within Phase I.

12 Copy the formula to Phase II and Phase III

workdays w/o holidays
51
50
64

Update the workbook

Time functions

Explanation

In Excel, the time of day is represented by the numbers following the decimal point in a date serial number. The number can range from 0 to 0.99999999.

- 0 represents 0:00:00, which is 12:00 AM
- .99999999 represents 23:59:59, which is 11:59 PM

NOW

The NOW function returns the current date and time, separated by a decimal point.

```
=NOW()
```

Subtracting times

To find the difference between a start time and an end time, you can use a simple subtraction formula. When you're using times in formulas, it's important to have the appropriate cell format applied. The Time format will display the time as *hh:mm:ss AM/PM*. If you want to see the results in terms of the number of hours, you need to apply the Number or General format.

For example, when given the start and end times of a project, you can calculate the number of hours spent working on that project by using the following formula:

```
=(end_time-start_time)*24
```

Multiplying the result by 24 determines the value in hours.

Do it!

B-2: Using time functions

Here's how	Here's why
1 Click the **Hours worked** tab	You'll create a formula that calculates the number of hours each employee worked.
2 Observe B3	The In column contains the time that the employee started working today. The cell is formatted as Time.
Observe C3	This is the amount of time that the employee took for lunch. This cell is formatted as Number.
Observe D3	The Out column contains the time that the employee clocked out for the day. Again, the cell is formatted as Time.
3 In E3, enter **=(D3-B3)*24**	To subtract the start time from the end time to find the time difference, and then multiply by 24 to find the value in hours.
Enter **−C3**	✗ ✓ *fx* =(D3-B3)*24-C3 To subtract the time spent on a lunch break.
Press (↵ ENTER)	Because column E is formatted as Time, the result is not exactly what you want.
4 Apply the Number format to E3		In	Lunch (in hours)	Out	Total Hours
---	---	---	---
8:00 AM	0.50	5:00 PM	8.50	 This employee worked a total of 8.5 hours.
5 Calculate the total hours worked for the other employees	**Total Hours** 8.50 8.50 8.33 8.50 9.00 9.75 8.50 9.00 8.63 9.25 Drag the fill handle to copy the formula.
6 Update and close the workbook	

Topic C: Array formulas

This topic covers the following Microsoft Office Specialist objectives for exam 77-888: Excel Expert 2010.

#	Objective
2.3	**Perform data summary tasks**
	2.3.1 Use an array formula
2.4	**Apply functions in formulas**
	2.4.3 Apply arrays to functions

Using array formulas

Explanation

The most basic definition of an *array* is a collection of values. Often, arrays are defined by cell references. However, arrays can also be groups of raw data or values. In this case, the arrays would be referred to as *array constants*.

An *array formula* performs multiple calculations on one or more sets of values, and then returns either a single result or multiple results. For example, as shown in Exhibit 2-1, you can create one array formula that calculates the Total sales for each product by multiplying the Unit price (B7:B19) by the Units sold (C7:C19) and entering the result in the range D7:D19. In this example, B7:B19 is an array, and C7:C19 is another array.

Creating array formulas

The syntax for array formulas is the same as any other Excel formula. You start with an equal sign (=), and you can use any built-in Excel function. You must press Ctrl+Shift+Enter to enter the formula. Array formulas are enclosed in braces {}. You cannot manually enter the braces to create an array formula.

Array formulas offer several advantages:

- **Consistency** — Because the same formula is entered in the destination range, verifying the accuracy of the formula is easier.
- **Editing safeguards** — When arrays involve multiple cells, you cannot edit just one of the cells. You must select the entire array, modify it, and then press Ctrl+Shift+Enter to confirm the change in the formula.
- **Reduced file size** — When a single array formula replaces multiple individual formulas, Excel needs to store only the single array formula. The more individual formulas replaced by the array formula, the greater the reduction in file size.

D7		▾	fx	{=B7:B19*C7:C19}	

	A	B	C	D
1	**Outlander Spices**			
2	**Inventory**			
3				
4				
5				
6	**Product**	**Unit price**	**Units sold**	**Total Sales**
7	Angelica Root	13.60	500	6800
8	Anise	3.34	2500	8350
9	Anise Seeds	19.54	430	8402.2
10	Annatto Seed	2.25	348	783
11	Asafoetida Powder	12.23	630	7704.9
12	Basil Leaf (Ground)	51.29	150	7693.5
13	Basil Leaf (Whole)	31.75	520	16510
14	Caraway Seed (Ground)	31.78	195	6197.1
15	Caraway Seed (Whole)	53.12	184	9774.08
16	Cardamom Seed (Ground)	24.37	190	4630.3
17	Cardamom Seed (Whole)	54.74	250	13685
18	Carob Powder (Raw)	1.50	855	1282.5
19	Cassia	9.87	580	5724.6
20				

Exhibit 2-1: Creating an array formula in D7:D19

Do it!

C-1:   Using an array formula

The files for this activity are in Student Data folder **Unit 2\Topic C**.

Here's how	Here's why
1 Open Inventory	
Save the workbook as **My Inventory**	
2 Select D7:D19	You will create an array that calculates the total sales for each product (Unit price*Units sold). The first step is to select the destination range.
3 Enter **=B7:B19*C7:C19**	To multiply the unit prices by the units sold for each product. You can type or select the ranges B7:B19 and C7:C19.
4 Press ⸤CTRL⸥ + ⸤SHIFT⸥ + ⸤↵ ENTER⸥	To enter the formula as an array formula. Excel encloses the array formula in braces. You can create an array formula only by pressing Ctrl+Shift+Enter; you cannot manually insert the braces.
5 Select the cells in D7:D19	f_x {=B7:B19*C7:C19} All cells contain the same array formula; however, the result of the calculation is different for each product.
6 Update the workbook	

Applying arrays to functions

Explanation

In addition to creating an array formula that returns multiple results, you can create an array formula that returns a single result, as shown in Exhibit 2-2. For example, you can use the SUM function to calculate the total sales of all products. In this case, you will use an array with the SUM function.

Use the following steps to create a SUM function using an array as the arguments:

1   Select the cell where you want the formula to be placed.
2   Type =**SUM(**
3   Enter (or select) the array to be used as the first argument.
4   Type *
5   Enter (or select) the array to be used as the second argument. Type the closing parenthesis.
6   Press Ctrl+Shift+Enter.

	B21	▾	f_x {=SUM(B7:B19*C7:C19)}	
	A	B	C	D
1	**Outlander Spices**			
2	**Inventory**			
3				
4				
5				
6	Product	Unit price	Units sold	Total Sales
7	Angelica Root	13.60	500	6800
8	Anise	3.34	2500	8350
9	Anise Seeds	19.54	430	8402.2
10	Annatto Seed	2.25	348	783
11	Asafoetida Powder	12.23	630	7704.9
12	Basil Leaf (Ground)	51.29	150	7693.5
13	Basil Leaf (Whole)	31.75	520	16510
14	Caraway Seed (Ground)	31.78	195	6197.1
15	Caraway Seed (Whole)	53.12	184	9774.08
16	Cardamom Seed (Ground)	24.37	190	4630.3
17	Cardamom Seed (Whole)	54.74	250	13685
18	Carob Powder (Raw)	1.50	855	1282.5
19	Cassia	9.87	580	5724.6
20				
21	Grand Total	$97,537.18		

Exhibit 2-2: Creating an array formula that returns a single result

Do it!

C-2: Applying arrays to functions

Here's how	Here's why
1 Select B21	You will enter an array formula that calculations the grand total sales for the products.
2 Enter **=SUM(B7:B19*C7:C19)**	To create a SUM function and use the array as the arguments.
3 Press (CTRL) + (SHIFT) + (↵ ENTER)	To create the array formula that will return a single result.
4 Observe the formula	The Grand Total in B21 is $97,537.18.
5 In D20, click [Σ]	To verify that the result is the same as the result in B21. Even though the range D7:D19 contains the array formula, the AutoSum function uses the values in its calculation.
Delete the formula in D20	
6 Update the workbook	

Modifying array formulas

Explanation

As stated earlier, you cannot delete or modify the contents of a cell that is included in a multi-cell array unless you edit the entire array. A common change is to add or remove rows that are included in the array formula. To do so, use the following technique:

1 Select the cell containing the array formula to be modified.
2 Press F2 to activate Edit mode. The braces temporarily disappear.
3 Edit the cell references as needed.
4 Press Ctrl+Shift+Enter to enter the modified array formula.

C-3: Modifying the array formula

Here's how	Here's why
1 Move A21:B21 down to A29:B29	To make space to add more products.
2 Click the **More products** tab	This sheet contains eight additional products with unit price and units sold information that you want to include on the Inventory tab.

Select A2:C9 and click

	A	B	C
1	**Product**	**Unit price**	**Units sold**
2	Celery Seed (Ground)	12.40	200
3	Chamomile Flowers	3.34	351
4	Chili Pepper Powder	10.50	520
5	Chinese Star Anise (Whole)	2.25	89
6	Chives	12.23	485
7	Cilantro Flakes	15.00	498
8	Cloves (Ground)	31.75	295
9	Coarse Kosher Salt Flakes	25.00	328

To copy the information for the eight additional products.

3 Click the **Inventory** tab	.
Select A20 and click	To paste the additional products.
4 Observe the error indicator in B29	Excel recognizes that a change affecting the formula has occurred.

$97,537.18

The formula in this cell refers to a range that has additional numbers adjacent to it.

5 Press F2	To activate Edit mode as indicated in the status bar. The braces temporarily disappear as you edit the formula.
6 In the formula bar, change B19 to **B27**	To include the new products.
Change C19 to **C27**	The additional rows are included in the array arguments.
7 Press CTRL + SHIFT + ↵ ENTER	
	To enter the modified array formula. The array formula is enclosed in braces again.
8 Select D7:D27	You must select the entire array to modify the array formula.
Activate Edit mode and change the cell references to **B27** and **C27**	Press F2, and edit the cell references in the formula bar.

9 Press [CTRL] + [SHIFT] + [↵ ENTER]

f_x | {=B7:B27*C7:C27}

To enter the modified array formula.

10 Update and close the workbook

Topic D: Displaying and printing formulas

This topic covers the following Microsoft Office Specialist objectives for exam 77-888: Excel Expert 2010.

#	Objective
2.2	**Manipulate formula options**
	2.2.1 Set iterative calculation options
	2.2.2 Enable or disable automatic workbook calculations

Viewing formulas in a worksheet

Explanation

You can display the formulas in a worksheet rather than their results. This is helpful when you want to audit your formulas.

There are two ways to display formulas in a worksheet:

- On the Formulas tab, in the Formula Auditing group, click Show Formulas.
- Press Ctrl + ` (accent grave).

Once the formulas are displayed in a worksheet, they can also be printed. To display the formula results again, click Show Formulas or press Ctrl + `.

Hiding formulas

There's a difference between not displaying formulas and hiding them. When you choose not to display formulas, the formula will still appear in the formula bar when you select the cell that shows that formula's result.

You can also hide formulas from users. This is useful when you want to prevent the formulas from being edited. A hidden formula will not be shown in the formula bar even when the associated cell is selected.

To hide a formula:

1 Select the cells whose formulas you want to hide. These can be adjacent or not, and you can select the whole sheet.
2 On the Home tab, in the Cells group, click Format and choose Format Cells.
3 Click the Protection tab, check Hidden and click OK.
4 On the Home tab, in the Cells group, click Format and choose Protect Sheet.
5 Ensure that the "Protect worksheet and contents of locked cells" box is checked.
6 Click OK.

To show formulas that were previously hidden, you need to remove protection. Here's how:

1 On the Review tab, in the Changes group, click Unprotect Sheet.
2 Select the range of cells whose formulas you want to unhide.
3 On the Home tab, in the Cells group, click Format and choose Format Cells.
4 Click the Protection tab, clear the Hidden checkbox and click OK.

Do it! **D-1: Showing, printing, and hiding formulas**

The files for this activity are in Student Data folder **Unit 2\Topic D**.

Here's how	Here's why
1 Open Targets	
Save the workbook as **My targets**	In the current topic folder.
2 Click the ROUND sheet	You'll display the formulas in this sheet.
3 Select C5	
Observe the formula bar	f_x =ROUND(B5*140%,-4)
	It shows the formula, while C5 shows the result of that formula.
4 Press CTRL + `	(The accent grave is usually to the left of the number 1 on the keyboard.) To display formulas in the cells.
Observe the Target sales column	Target sales for current year =ROUND(B5*140%,-4) =ROUND(B6*140%,-4) =ROUND(B7*140%,-4) =ROUND(B8*140%,-4) =ROUND(B9*140%,-4) =ROUND(B10*140%,-4) =ROUND(B11*140%,-4) =ROUND(B12*140%,-4) =ROUND(B13*140%,-4) =ROUND(B14*140%,-4) =ROUND(B15*140%,-4) =ROUND(B16*140%,-4) =ROUND(B17*140%,-4) =ROUND(B18*140%,-4)
	It now shows the formulas instead of the results.
5 Click the **File** tab	
Click **Print**	
Observe the Target sales column in the print preview	(Move to the second page and zoom in, if necessary.) Formulas will be printed instead of the formulas' results. This can be handy for auditing the formulas.
6 Click the **Formulas** tab	You won't print at this time.
Click **Show Formulas**	To switch from displaying the formulas to displaying the formula results.
7 Select C5 to C18	You'll hide the formulas in these cells.

8	On the Home tab, click **Format** and choose **Format Cells...**	(In the Cells group.) To open the Format Cells dialog box.
	Click the **Protection** tab	The cells are locked.
	Check **Hidden**	Note that the locked and hidden settings will not take effect until you protect the sheet.
	Click **OK**	To close the Format Cells dialog box and return to the worksheet.
9	On the Review tab, click **Protect Sheet**	(In the Changes group.) To open the Protect Sheet dialog box.
	Check **Protect worksheet and contents of locked cells**	(If necessary.) You can leave the password box empty.
	Click **OK**	To close the Protect Sheet dialog box.
10	Select C5	The formula does not appear in the formula bar; however, the results still appear in the worksheet.
11	Try to edit any cell in the range C5:C18	Press any letter or number while any cell in the range is selected. A message appears, telling you that the cell is protected and therefore read-only.
	Click **OK**	To close the message box.
12	Unprotect the sheet	On the Review tab, in the Changes group, click Unprotect Sheet.
	Observe the formula bar	You can now see the formulas in C5:C18.
13	Update the workbook	

Disabling automatic calculation of formulas

Explanation

Workbook formulas are automatically calculated when any cell that relates to the formula is changed. When a workbook contains numerous formulas, the automatic recalculation might be time consuming and cumbersome as you work in the file. You can disable the automatic recalculation and manually calculate the workbook formulas when you want.

To disable automatic calculation of formulas, use the following procedure:

1 Click the File tab and choose Options.

2 Select Formulas.

3 Under Calculation options, select Manual. By default, the workbook will be recalculated before it is saved.

4 Click OK.

To manually calculate the formulas, press F9 or click the Calculate Now button in the Calculations group on the Formulas tab.

Iteration is the repeated recalculation of worksheet formulas until the maximum number of calculations is reached. A *circular reference* is created when a formula refers to the cell containing the formula. The calculation of a circular reference can go on forever. You can change Excel calculation settings to avoid indefinite recalculations.

To change the iterative calculation options:

1 In the Excel Options dialog box, select Formulas.

2 Under Calculation options, check "Enable iterative calculation."

3 In the Maximum Iterations box, specify the number of iterations allowed. The higher the number, the longer the recalculation will take.

4 In the Maximum Change box, specify the acceptable amount of change between recalculations. The smaller the number, the more time the recalculation will take but the more accurate the result will be.

5 Click OK.

Do it!

D-2: Setting calculation options

The files for this activity are in Student Data folder **Unit 2\Topic D**.

Here's how	Here's why
1 Click the **File** tab and choose **Options**	To open the Excel Options dialog box.
2 Select **Formulas**	To display the options related to formulas, calculations, and error handling.
3 Under "Calculation options," observe the default setting	By default, Excel automatically recalculates formulas when there is a change in any of the cells that affect the formula. To avoid having to wait for your workbook formulas to recalculate, you can specify manual calculation.
4 Select **Manual**	Calculation options Workbook Calculation ⓘ 　◯ Automatic 　◯ Automatic except for data tables 　◉ Manual 　　　☑ Recalculate workbook before saving By default, Excel will recalculate the workbook before it is saved.
5 Check **Enable iterative calculation**	☑ Enable iterative calculation 　Maximum Iterations: 100 　Maximum Change: 0.001 By default, the maximum number of iterations is 100, with an acceptable change of 0.001.
6 Click **OK**	To save the changed settings.
7 Update and close the workbook	

Unit summary: Financial and date functions

Topic A   In this topic, you used the **PMT function** to calculate periodic payments for a loan.

Topic B   In this topic, you used **date** functions to calculate the difference between two dates. You created a Time formula to determine the number of hours worked.

Topic C   In this topic, you created an **array formula** that performed multiple calculations on multiple data sets to obtain multiple results. You also created an array formula using a SUM function.

Topic D   In this topic, you learned how to display, print, and hide **formulas**. You changed the **calculation settings** and iteration limits for your Excel worksheets.

Independent practice activity

In this activity, you'll enter calculations, such as a nested IF function.

The files for this activity are in Student Data folder **Unit 2\Unit summary**.

1 Open Loan statement.

2 Save the workbook as **My Loan statement**.

3 Activate the Loan statement worksheet and calculate the quarterly amount to be paid to all of the institutions. (*Hint:* You'll need to divide the interest rate by 4 instead of 12. Scroll down to cell A101 to see the correct formula.) Copy the formula to E6:E9. If necessary, increase the column width to display the full results.

4 Compare your results with Exhibit 2-3.

5 Display the formulas in the cells.

6 Examine the formulas in Print Preview. Close the Print Preview when you're done.

7 Display the results of the formulas in the cells again.

8 Hide the formulas from users. (*Hint:* You need to format these cells as hidden and then protect the worksheet.) Test that the formulas are hidden and that you can't edit the cells.

9 Unprotect the worksheet.

10 Activate the Stocks worksheet and use a date function to enter the current date in F2.

11 Use the YEAR function to calculate the number of years that each stock has been owned. (*Hint:* Depending on the current date, your results for B5:D5 might be different.)

12 In B9, create an array formula that multiplies the Shares by the Share price for each stock and returns a single value. (*Hint:* Remember to press Ctrl+Shift+Enter.) Compare your worksheet to Exhibit 2-4.

13 Update and close the workbook.

Outlander Spices				
Statement of loan				
Institution	Loan amount (in $)	Period of repayment (in quarters)	Annual Rate of Interest (in %)	Quarterly payment
AmericaBank	$150,000	12	14	-$15,522.59
NewCiti	$325,000	16	15	-$27,379.57
StandardBank	$375,000	20	10	-$24,055.17
DoubleMoney	$450,000	20	15	-$32,382.94
WACA	$635,000	24	10	-$35,504.64
Total	$1,935,000			

Exhibit 2-3: The Loan statement sheet after Step 3

B5			f_x	=YEAR($F$2)-YEAR(B4)		
	A	B	C	D	E	F
1	Stock prices					Current date
2						10/21/2010
3		AEOR	JOET	OERR		
4	Date purchased	4/15/2000	8/20/1995	10/31/1985		
5	Years owned	10	15	25		
6	Shares	312	405	620		
7	Share price	12.34	15.25	20.25		
8						
9	Total stock value	$3,850.08				

Exhibit 2-4: The Stocks sheet after Step 12

Review questions

1 What function returns the periodic payments for a loan?

2 What date function inserts the current date?

3 What function inserts the current date and time?

4 How can you distinguish an array formula from a regular formula?

5 How do you enter an array formula?

Unit 3

Lookups and data tables

Complete this unit, and you'll know how to:

A Use the VLOOKUP and HLOOKUP functions to find values in a worksheet list.

B Use the MATCH function to find the relative position of a value in a range, and use the INDEX function to find the value of a cell at a given position within a range.

C Use data tables to see the effects of changing the values in a formula.

Topic A: Using lookup functions

Explanation

You can find a value in a range of related data in a worksheet by using *lookup functions*. These functions find a value in the first row or column of a list and then return a corresponding value from another row or column.

HLOOKUP and VLOOKUP

The HLOOKUP function performs a horizontal lookup. It finds values in a lookup table that has row labels in the leftmost column. The VLOOKUP function performs a vertical lookup. It finds values in a lookup table that has column labels in the topmost row.

HLOOKUP searches for the lookup value in the first row of the lookup table and returns a value in the same column from the specified row of the table. The syntax is:

```
HLOOKUP(lookup_value,table_array,row_index_num,range_lookup)
```

In this syntax:

- `lookup_value` is located in the first row of the lookup table.
- `table_array` is the name of the lookup table range.
- `row_index_num` is the number of the row from which a value will be returned.
- `range_lookup` is an optional argument that specifies whether you want HLOOKUP to find an exact or approximate match. You can specify FALSE if you want the function to search for a value that falls within a range, or specify TRUE if you want the function to search for an approximate match. If you omit the argument, HLOOKUP assumes that the value is TRUE.

Similarly, VLOOKUP searches for the lookup value in the first column of the lookup table and returns a value in the same row from the specified column of the table. The syntax is:

```
VLOOKUP(lookup_value,table_array,col_index_num,range_lookup)
```

In this syntax:

- `lookup_value` is located in the first column of the lookup table.
- `table_array` is the name of the lookup table range.
- `col_index_num` is the number of the column from which a value will be returned.
- `range_lookup` is an optional argument that specifies whether you want VLOOKUP to find an exact or approximate match. If you omit the argument, VLOOKUP assumes that the value is TRUE.

Do it!   ## A-1: Examining VLOOKUP

The files for this activity are in Student Data folder **Unit 3\Topic A**.

Here's how	Here's why
1 Open Employees	This workbook contains seven worksheets; Lookup is the active sheet. The data in the Lookup worksheet is sorted in ascending order by the values in the Employee ID column. The range A4:E6 contains a search box that currently displays the name and department for the employee identification number E001.
2 Save the workbook as **My employees**	In the current topic folder.
3 Verify that the Lookup sheet is active	
In A6, enter **E037**	The name and department details of Employee ID E037 appear in B6 and C6, respectively. Entering an incorrect identification number in A6 would create errors in B6 and C6.
4 Select B6	It contains a VLOOKUP function that finds the name of the employee whose identification number is specified in A6.
Observe the formula bar	*f͙x* =VLOOKUP(A6,Emp_info,2,FALSE)
	In this formula, "A6" refers to the cell containing the value that the function has to find. "Emp_info" is the range A10:F49, which constitutes the lookup table. The "2" refers to the table column from which the matching value is returned. "FALSE" indicates that the function must find an exact match.
	In the row containing E037, the value in the second column of the lookup table is Davis Lee.
5 Select C6	*f͙x* =VLOOKUP(A6,Emp_info,5,FALSE)
	It contains a VLOOKUP function that finds the department of the person whose employee identification number appears in A6.
6 Update the workbook	

Using VLOOKUP to find exact matches

Explanation

When you use the VLOOKUP function, remember the following:

- The lookup value must always be located in the first column of the lookup table.
- If the range_lookup argument is TRUE, the values in the first column of the lookup range must be in ascending order.
- Uppercase and lowercase text are equivalent.

Do it!

A-2: Using VLOOKUP to find an exact match

Here's how	Here's why
1 Select D6	You'll use the VLOOKUP function to find the earnings of the employee whose ID is entered in A6.
Enter **=VLOOKUP(A6,Emp_info,6,FALSE)**	
	The value 72500 appears.
2 In E6, enter **=VLOOKUP(A6,Emp_info,4,FALSE)**	
	The value East appears. This is the region of the employee whose ID is entered in A6.
3 In A6, enter **E029**	The employee details appear as shown.
4 Update the workbook	

Using VLOOKUP to find approximate matches

Explanation

You can also use the VLOOKUP function to return an approximate match. To do this, specify the range_lookup argument as TRUE. If the function doesn't find an exact match, it looks for the largest value that is less than the lookup value and returns its corresponding data. This is also the default value if you leave the argument blank.

If the lookup value is less than the smallest value in the table, an error (#N/A) is returned.

Do it!

A-3:   Using VLOOKUP to find an approximate match

Here's how	Here's why
1 Click the VLOOKUP sheet	This table lists discount percentages corresponding to purchase amounts. Because there are so many levels of discounts, it would be impractical to calculate the percentage with a large nested IF function. Instead, you'll find the nearest discount percentage based on an approximate matching lookup.
2 Select B6	You'll use the VLOOKUP function to find the discount percentage for the amount entered in A6. The table correlating purchase amounts to discounts is named Discount_table.
Enter **=VLOOKUP(A6,Discount_table,2,TRUE)**	
	Because the value in A6 is $1000, the lookup formula in B6 results in 3%, matching the data in the lookup table.
	You'll now enter a purchase amount value that doesn't appear in the table. The TRUE value in the last argument of the function tells VLOOKUP to look for an approximate match instead of an exact match.
3 In A6, enter **2500**	The discount for a $2000 purchase is 10%, and the discount for a $3500 purchase is 12%. The largest amount in the lookup table below your entry of $2500 is $2000, so the discount should be 10%. Because the VLOOKUP function is looking for an approximate match, it determines this and returns a discount value of 10%.
4 Update the workbook	

Using HLOOKUP to find exact matches

Explanation

HLOOKUP works like VLOOKUP except that it searches for values along a row instead of down a column. When you use the HLOOKUP function, remember the following:

- The lookup value must always be located in the first row of the lookup table.
- If the range_lookup argument is TRUE (approximate search), the values in the first row of the lookup range must be in ascending order.
- Uppercase and lowercase text are equivalent.

Search	Profit Information		
Region	Gross Profit	Net Profit	% Profit
Qtr2	$36,150.00	$22,000.00	28.00%

Exhibit 3-1: Using HLOOKUP

Do it!

A-4: Using HLOOKUP to find exact matches

Here's how	Here's why
1 Click the HLOOKUP-Exact sheet	You'll add formulas for horizontal lookups.
2 Select B5	A drop-down arrow appears.
3 Click the drop-down arrow and select **Qtr2**	Corresponding data is displayed in C5. The list ensures that you enter valid data.
4 Select C5	
Observe the formula	It is similar to the VLOOKUP formula, but it searches the first row in table_array rather than the first column.
5 Select D5	
Enter **=HLOOKUP(B5,total_sales,9,FALSE)**	
	The row_index is 9, which is the row for Net profit. FALSE indicates a search for an exact match.
6 Select E5	
Enter the formula to show Profit % for the selected quarter	Enter =HLOOKUP(B5,total_sales,10,FALSE). The row_index for Profit % is 10.
7 Update the workbook	Compare your worksheet to Exhibit 3-1.

Using HLOOKUP to find approximate matches

Explanation

You can also use the HLOOKUP function to return an approximate match. To do this, specify the `range_lookup` argument as TRUE. As with VLOOKUP, if the HLOOKUP function doesn't find an exact match, it looks for the largest value that is less than the lookup value and returns its corresponding data. This is also the default value if you leave the argument blank.

If the lookup value is less than the smallest value in the table, an error (#N/A) is returned. The data in the first row must be in ascending order. If it's not, the function might return unexpected results.

Do it!

A-5: Using HLOOKUP to find approximate matches

Here's how	Here's why
1 Click the HLOOKUP-Approx sheet	
2 Select C4	

B	C
Search	
Earnings	Name
$66,000	

You will enter an HLOOKUP function to find an approximate match.

Enter
=HLOOKUP(B4,base_salary,2,TRUE)

TRUE indicates an approximate search.

3 Select B4

Enter an amount between 60,000 and 80,000

You don't need to enter the comma or dollar sign. The function finds the largest value that is less than or equal to the entered value and returns the corresponding name.

Update and close the workbook

Topic B: Using MATCH and INDEX

Explanation

The MATCH and INDEX functions are considered Reference functions. You can use the MATCH function to determine the relative position of a value in a range. Conversely, the INDEX function returns a cell's value based on its relative position in a range. You can combine these two functions to obtain any information from any table.

The MATCH function

The syntax of the MATCH function is:

```
MATCH(lookup_value,lookup_array,match_type)
```

The arguments are:

- `lookup_value` — The value you want to find.
- `lookup_array` — The range of cells containing possible lookup values.
- `match_type` — An optional argument that can have the values 0, 1, or -1. If you want an exact match, use 0. If you want the function to search for the largest value that is less than or equal to the lookup value, use 1. If you want the function to search for the smallest value that is greater than or equal to the lookup value, use -1.

  If you use 1, the range should be sorted in ascending order. If you use -1, the range should be sorted in descending order. If you omit the argument, the function assumes that the value is 1.

Do it!

B-1: Using the MATCH function

The files for this activity are in Student Data folder **Unit 3\Topic B**.

Here's how	Here's why
1 Open Earnings	
Save the workbook as **My earnings**	In the current topic folder.
2 Click the Match and Index sheet	The data appears in ascending order of earnings. You'll use the MATCH function to find the relative position of a value in the selected range. The ranges A4:B7 and E4:F6 contain search boxes.
3 Select B6	**Search based on name**
		Enter name	Sandy Stewart	
		Relative position		
		Earnings		
	You'll find the relative position of "Sandy Stewart" in the column of names.
Enter **=MATCH(B5,Emp_name,0)**	In this formula, "B5" refers to the cell containing the lookup value. "Emp_name" refers to the range B10:B49, where the function searches for the lookup value. The "0" indicates that the values in the search range should match the lookup value exactly.
	The value 4 appears in B6. This is the relative position of "Sandy Stewart" in the column of names. In other words, her name is the fourth name in the list.
4 Select F6	**Search based on earnings**
		Enter earnings	$100,000	
		Relative position		
	You'll find the relative position of the value in F5 within the range F10:F49, named Earnings.
Enter **=MATCH(F5,Earnings,1)**	In this formula, "1" indicates that the function will find the largest value that is less than or equal to the lookup value.
	The relative position of the value in F5 appears as 24 in F6. The range named Earnings contains 24 values that are less than or equal to $100,000.
Observe the Earnings column	It doesn't contain the value $100,000. However, MATCH still displays a relative position in F6. This occurs because MATCH returns the relative position of the largest value that's less than or equal to $100,000.
5 Update the workbook	

The INDEX function

Explanation

You can use the INDEX function if you want to find a value in a range by specifying a row number and a column number. The syntax of the INDEX function is:

    INDEX(range,row_num,col_num)

The arguments are:

- `range` — The group of cells in which to look for the value.
- `row_num` — The row from which a value will be returned. If the specified range contains only one row, you can omit the row number.
- `col_num` — The column from which a value will be returned. If the specified range contains only one column, you can omit the column number.

For example, `INDEX(A1:F10,4,6)` returns the value in row 4 and column 6 of the range A1:F10.

By itself, the INDEX function isn't very useful; the person looking for data isn't likely to know which row and column values to enter. When used with the MATCH function, however, the INDEX function can return values that the VLOOKUP function can't. VLOOKUP always looks for a matching value in the *leftmost* column of a data range. If you want to match a value in another column, you can use the MATCH function to return the row that matches the user's input, and then use that result in an INDEX function.

For example, in Exhibit 3-2, cell B6 contains a MATCH function to determine the row for the name entered in B5. Sandy Stewart is the fourth name in the Emp_info list. Cell B7 contains an INDEX function that looks in the row specified in B6 (in this case, row 4) and returns the value of the sixth column (Earnings, in this case, $65,000).

B7		f_x	=INDEX(Emp_info,B6,6)			
	A	B	C	D	E	F
1			**Outlander Spices**			
2			**Employee information**			
3						
4	Search based on name				Search based on earnings	
5	**Enter name**	Sandy Stewart			**Enter earnings**	$100,000
6	**Relative position**	4			**Relative position**	24
7	**Earnings**	$65,000				
8						
9	Employee identification number	Name	SSN	Region	Department	Earnings
10	E006	Annie Philips	000-85-8586	West	Human resources	$60,000
11	E030	Diana Stone	000-51-2998	East	Marketing	$60,000
12	E019	Jamie Morrison	000-35-4665	East	Human resources	$62,000
13	E033	Sandy Stewart	000-39-8005	East	Marketing	$65,000
14	E014	Michael Lee	000-87-9898	North	Sales	$68,000
15	E031	Rob Dukes	000-64-6797	West	Accounts	$70,000
16	E001	Malcolm Pingault	000-17-3312	East	Human resources	$72,000
17	E037	Davis Lee	000-28-7743	East	Accounts	$72,500

Exhibit 3-2: The INDEX function used with the MATCH function

Do it!

B-2: Using the INDEX function

Here's how	Here's why
1 Observe B7	You want to display the salary for the employee whose name is entered in cell B5. You can't use the VLOOKUP function for this because the person's name is in the second column of the data table, not the first column.
	You'll begin by experimenting with the INDEX function, which you'll use to solve this problem.
2 Select B7	You'll enter row and column values directly into the formula this time to see how the INDEX function works.
Enter **=INDEX(Emp_info,2,6)**	In this formula, "Emp_info" refers to the range A10:F49. The "2" and "6" refer to the row and column from which the function should return a value.
	The value $60,000 appears in B7. This is the value from the second row and sixth column of the specified range.
	You'll now replace the number 2 with the value from cell B6, which represents the row of the entered name (calculated by using the MATCH function).
3 Select B7	
Edit the formula to read **=INDEX(Emp_info,B6,6)**	As shown in Exhibit 3-2, the value $65,000 appears in B7. Because B6 contains the value 4 (the row number for Sandy Stewart), the value in column 6 that the INDEX function returns is her salary.
4 Select B5	You'll verify that the functions work when you enter a different name.
Enter **Davis Lee**	Search based on name
		Enter name	Davis Lee	
		Relative position	8	
		Earnings	$72,500	
	The MATCH function in B6 calculates the relative position of 8, and the INDEX function in B7 calculates the salary of $72,500.
5 Update and close the workbook	

Topic C: Creating data tables

Explanation

A *data table* is a range that displays the results of changing certain values in one or more formulas. The different values you want to enter in a formula are also included in the data table. A data table can have either a single variable or two variables.

One-variable data tables

You can use a one-variable data table to observe the effects of changing one variable in one or more formulas. For example, you can see how changing the interest rate affects monthly payments in the function PMT(A5%/12,36,12000). In this function, A5 is called the *input cell*, where various input values are substituted from the data table.

To create a one-variable data table:

1 Enter input values in a row or a column.

2 If you list the input values in a column, then enter the formula in the cell located at the intersection of the row above the first input value and the column to the right of the input values, as shown in Exhibit 3-3. If you list the input values in a row, then enter the formula in the cell located at the intersection of the column to the left of the first value and the row just below the row of input values.

3 Select the range containing the input values and the formula.

4 On the Data tab, in the Data Tools group, click What-If Analysis and choose Data Table to open the Data Table dialog box.

5 If the input values are in a column, specify the input cell in the Column input cell box. If the input values are in a row, use the Row input cell box.

6 Click OK.

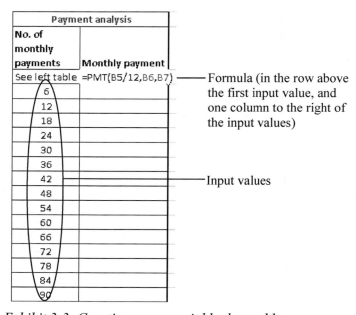

Exhibit 3-3: Creating a one-variable data table

Do it!

C-1: Creating a one-variable data table

The files for this activity are in Student Data folder **Unit 3\Topic C**.

Here's how	Here's why
1 Open Payments	
Save the workbook as **My payments**	In the current topic folder.
2 Click the 1v data table sheet	(If necessary.) You'll create a one-variable data table to analyze payments. D6:E21 will form the data table. The range D7:D21 contains the input values you'll use while creating the data table.
3 In E6, enter **=PMT(B5/12,B6,B7)**	To calculate monthly payments based on the input cell. The value -8,791.59 appears.
4 Select D6:E21	
5 Click the **Data** tab	
In the Data Tools group, click **What-If Analysis**	To display a menu.
Choose **Data Table...**	To open the Data Table dialog box. Here, you can specify the row and column input cells.
6 Place the insertion point in the Column input cell box	
Select B6	(In the worksheet.) This is the cell where the list of column input values from the data table will be substituted.

7 Click **OK**

Payment analysis	
No. of monthly payments	Monthly payment
See left table	-8,791.59
6	-17,156.14
12	-8,791.59
18	-6,005.71
24	-4,614.49
30	-3,781.14
36	-3,226.72
42	-2,831.68
48	-2,536.26
54	-2,307.24
60	-2,124.70
66	-1,975.97
72	-1,852.58
78	-1,748.69
84	-1,660.12
90	-1,583.79

(In the Data Table dialog box.) E6:E21 shows how different values for "No. of monthly payments" affect the monthly payment for the loan amount in B7. Because 12 appears in both the initial formula and the data table, the payment value of -8,791.59 appears twice.

You can change the initial value used in the formula without affecting the data table.

In B6, enter **10**

Payment analysis	
No. of monthly payments	Monthly payment
See left table	-10,464.04
6	-17,156.14
12	-8,791.59
18	-6,005.71
24	-4,614.49

The value in E6 (at the top of the data table) changes to -10,464.04, but the rest of the table values remain.

8 Update the workbook

Two-variable data tables

Explanation

You can use a two-variable data table to see the effect of changing two variables in one or more formulas, as shown in Exhibit 3-4. For example, you can see how changing the interest rate and the number of payments affects a monthly payment.

To create a two-variable data table:

1   Enter a formula that contains two input cells.
2   Below the formula (in the same column), enter the first list of input values. To the right of the formula (in the same row), enter the second list of input values.
3   Select the range containing both the input values and the formula.
4   In the Data Tools group, click What-If Analysis and choose Data Table to open the Data Table dialog box.
5   In the Row input cell box, specify the row input cell.
6   In the Column input cell box, specify the column input cell.
7   Click OK.

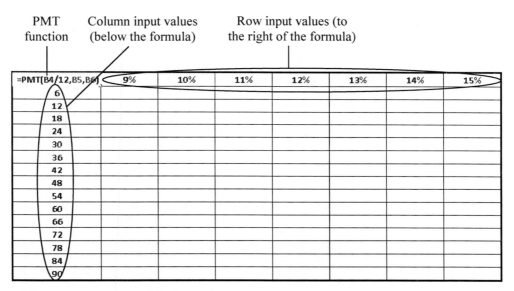

Exhibit 3-4: A two-variable data table

Do it!

C-2: Creating a two-variable data table

Here's how	Here's why
1 Click the 2v data table sheet	You'll create a two-variable data table to analyze monthly payments.
2 In B7, enter **=PMT(B4/12,B5,B6)**	To calculate monthly payments based on two input cells.
3 Select B7:I22	
Open the Data Table dialog box	(Click What-If Analysis and choose Data Table.) The insertion point is in the Row input cell box.
4 Select B4	To specify the row input cell.
Place the insertion point in the Column input cell box	
Select B5	To specify the column input cell.
5 Click **OK**	C8:I22 shows how different numbers of months and different interest rates affect the monthly payments for the loan amount in B6.
6 In B6, enter **250000**	The data table now shows payments based on a loan amount of $250,000.
7 Update and close the workbook	

Unit summary: Lookups and data tables

Topic A   In this topic, you learned that lookup functions are used to find specific values in a worksheet. You used the **VLOOKUP** function to search for a value in a list that is arranged vertically, and you used the **HLOOKUP** function to search for a value in a list that is arranged horizontally.

Topic B   In this topic, you used the **MATCH** function to find the relative position of a value in a range. You used the **INDEX** function to find a value in a range by specifying row and column numbers. You also used these two functions together to look up information more flexibly than you can with the VLOOKUP function.

Topic C   In this topic, you learned that a **data table** displays the effects of changing the values in a formula. You used a **one-variable** data table to observe the effect of changing one variable in a formula. You then used a **two-variable** data table to observe the effect of changing two variables in a formula.

Independent practice activity

In this activity, you'll use the VLOOKUP function to search for a value in a list that is arranged vertically. You'll also use the MATCH function, and you'll create a one-variable data table.

The files for this activity are in Student Data folder **Unit 3\Unit summary**.

1 Open City managers. (Ensure that Lookup is the active worksheet.)

2 Save the workbook as **My city managers**.

3 In B6, enter the VLOOKUP function that finds the manager of the city entered in A6. In C6, enter the VLOOKUP function that finds the phone number of the same manager. (*Hint:* The lookup table is named Contact_list. Scroll down to cell A100 to see the correct formulas for B6 and C6.)

4 Click the Match worksheet. In B6, use the MATCH function to find the number of managers with fewer accounts than the value entered in A6. (*Hint:* The accounts column is named Num_accounts. Scroll down to cell A100 to see the correct formula for B6.)

5 Click the 1v data table worksheet. In F6:G21, create a one-variable data table to calculate the monthly payments for the various payment schedules in F7:F21. Use the PMT function with an annual interest rate of 10%. Compare your results with Exhibit 3-7. (*Hint:* Scroll down to cell A100 to see the correct formula for G6.)

6 Update and close the workbook.

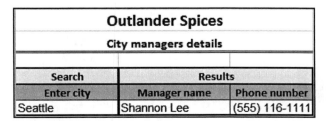

Exhibit 3-5: The results of the VLOOKUP function in Step 3

Outlander Spices	
City managers details	
Search	Results
Enter # of accounts	Number of managers with fewer than target
20	5

Exhibit 3-6: The results of the MATCH function in Step 4

Payment analysis	
No. of monthly payments	Monthly deduction
See left table	-728.55
6	-2,081.21
12	-1,066.51
18	-728.55
24	-559.78
30	-458.69
36	-391.43
42	-343.51
48	-307.67
54	-279.89
60	-257.75
66	-239.70
72	-224.74
78	-212.13
84	-201.39
90	-192.13

Exhibit 3-7: The results obtained after Step 5

Review questions

1 True or false? The VLOOKUP function is a vertical lookup function that finds values in a lookup table that has row labels in the leftmost column.

2 What is the syntax of the VLOOKUP function?

3 List three important points to remember about using the VLOOKUP function.

4 What is the purpose of the MATCH function?

5 What is a data table?

Unit 4

Advanced data management

Complete this unit, and you'll know how to:

A Use the data validation feature to validate data entered in cells.

B Use database functions to summarize data that meet the criteria you specify.

Topic A: Validating cell entries

This topic covers the following Microsoft Office Specialist objectives for exam 77-882: Excel 2010.

#	Objective
2.1	Construct cell data
	2.1.1 Use Paste Special
	2.1.1.9 Validation

This topic covers the following Microsoft Office Specialist objectives for exam 77-888: Excel Expert 2010.

#	Objective
2.1	Audit formulas
	2.1.4 Locate invalid data
2.4	Apply functions in formulas
	2.4.4 Use date functions

Validating data

Explanation

You can use Excel's data validation feature to ensure that selected cells accept only valid data, such as text, dates, or whole numbers. You can also ensure that users select only valid values from a specified list of options.

Validating data ensures that data entries match a specified format. You can display an input message that prompts users for the correct entries, and display a specific error message when incorrect data is entered.

To quickly see invalid data, you can display circles around invalid entries. To do so, click the Data tab, click the Data Validation button, and choose Circle Invalid Data. To remove the circles, click Data Validation and choose Clear Validation Circles.

Do it!   **A-1:   Observing data validation**

The files for this activity are in Student Data folder **Unit 4\Topic A**.

Here's how	Here's why
1 Open Details	The Observing data validation sheet is active. You'll observe the cells in which only certain kinds of data can be entered.
2 Save the workbook as **My details**	In the current topic folder.
3 Verify that the Observing data validation sheet is active	
4 Select B7, as shown	

4	Name	Emp_Id	Date of hire
5	Adam Long	E001	12/1/1997
6	Paul Anderson	E002	4/1/1998
7	Shannon Lee		
8			
9			Emp_Id
10			Employee identification number should be four characters long.
11			
12			

An input message appears, stating the acceptable format for Emp_Id numbers.

Enter **E1234**	The Invalid Emp_Id message box appears.

Invalid Emp_Id

The employee identification number you've entered is not allowed. Please enter another value.

[Retry]   [Cancel]   [Help]

Was this information helpful?

5 Click **Retry**	To close the message box.
Edit B7 to read **E003**	
Press (TAB)	The cell accepts the corrected Emp_Id.
6 In C7, enter tomorrow's date	(In mm/dd/yy format.) This date is not permitted because the date-of-hire value cannot be greater than today's date value. The "Invalid date of hire" message box appears.
Click **Cancel**	

7 Enter today's date	The cell accepts the corrected date.
8 Select D7	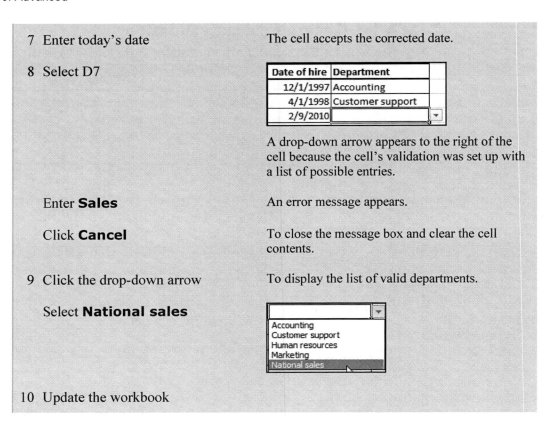
	A drop-down arrow appears to the right of the cell because the cell's validation was set up with a list of possible entries.
Enter **Sales**	An error message appears.
Click **Cancel**	To close the message box and clear the cell contents.
9 Click the drop-down arrow	To display the list of valid departments.
Select **National sales**	
10 Update the workbook	

Setting data validation rules

Explanation

To create a data validation rule:

1   Select the cells for which you want to create a validation rule.
2   On the Data tab, in the Data Tools group, click Data Validation to open the Data Validation dialog box, shown in Exhibit 4-1.
3   Click the Settings tab.
4   From the Allow list, select a data validation option.
5   From the Data list, select the operator you want to use. Then complete the remaining entries. (They will vary depending on the validation option and operator selected.)
6   On the Input Message tab, enter the message to be displayed when users select the cell.
7   On the Error Alert tab, enter the message to be displayed when users enter invalid data.
8   Click OK to set the validation rule and close the dialog box.

Pasting validation rules

You can use Paste Special to paste validation rules from one cell or range to another. To do so, select the range containing the validation rule you want to copy and click Copy. Then select the destination range, right-click, and choose Paste Special. In the Paste Special dialog box, select Validation and click OK.

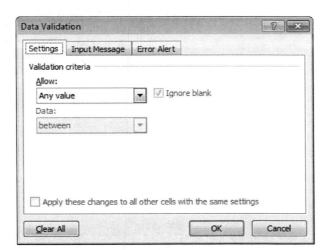

Exhibit 4-1: The Data Validation dialog box

Do it!

A-2: Creating a data validation rule

Here's how	Here's why
1 Click the Setting up data validation sheet	
2 Select B5	You'll create a validation rule to ensure that employee numbers are four characters long.
3 In the Data Tools group, click **Data Validation**	(On the Data tab.) To open the Data Validation dialog box, shown in Exhibit 4-1. By default, the Settings tab is active.
4 From the Allow list, select **Text length**	You will specify the number of characters permitted in each cell of the selected range. The Data list and the Minimum and Maximum boxes appear in the dialog box. The Ignore blank option also becomes available.
From the Data list, select **equal to**	To specify the comparison operator. The Length box replaces the Minimum and Maximum boxes.
In the Length box, enter **4**	To specify the number of characters permitted.

5 Click the **Input Message** tab	You'll specify the message that will appear when users select a cell in the Emp_Id column.
In the Title box, enter **Emp_Id**	This text will appear as a title in the input message.
In the Input message box, enter **Employee ID number should be four characters long.**	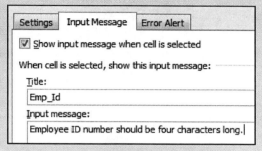
	This message will appear when the user selects a cell.
6 Click the **Error Alert** tab	
In the Title box, enter **Invalid Emp_Id**	This will be the title of the error message box.
In the Error message box, enter **The employee ID number you've entered is not permitted. Please enter another value.**	This is the error message that'll appear when the user enters an invalid employee identification number.
7 Display the Style list	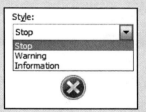
	To see the three types of error messages: Stop, Warning, and Information. Each error alert has its own corresponding icon.
Close the Style list	To leave the error alert style as Stop.
Click **OK**	To set the validation rule.
8 Select **B5**	The input message appears.
9 Enter **103**	The Invalid Emp_Id message box appears because you entered only three characters.
Click **Retry**	Or press Enter.
Enter **E103**	

10 Right-click B5 and choose **Copy**

Select B6:B20

Right-click and choose **Paste Special...**

Select **Validation**

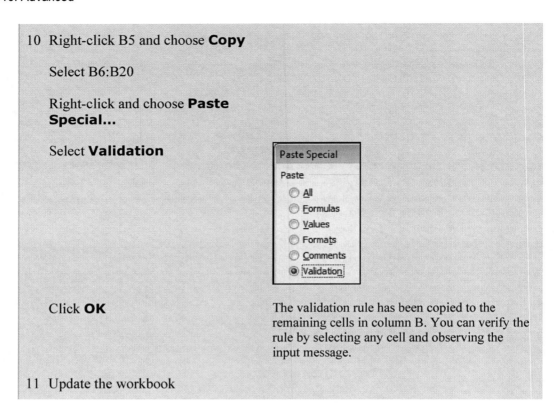

Click **OK**

The validation rule has been copied to the remaining cells in column B. You can verify the rule by selecting any cell and observing the input message.

11 Update the workbook

Using date and list criteria in data validation rules

Explanation

In addition to using text-length data validation, you can use date and list criteria in your data validation rules.

To specify date criteria for valid data:

1   Select the cells you want to validate.
2   On the Data tab, click Data Validation.
3   On the Settings tab in the Data Validation dialog box, select Date from the Allow list.
4   From the Data list, select the operator you want to use.
5   Complete the remaining criteria entries. When specifying dates, you can enter formulas that return dates, such as =TODAY().

  Note: The TODAY function returns the current date; the NOW function returns the current date and time.

6   Define an input message and an error message, if desired.
7   Click OK.

To specify list criteria for valid data:

1   Select the cells you want to validate.
2   Click Data Validation.
3   On the Settings tab, select List from the Allow list.
4   In the Source box, enter the desired list items, separated by a comma. List items are case sensitive. To edit items in the Source box, use the Backspace key or click the mouse.

  Note: You can also enter a cell or range reference instead of typing the list items.

5   Define an input message and an error message, if desired.
6   Click OK.

The width of the cell containing the data validation rule determines the width of the drop-down list. You can increase the width of the cell to make sure that longer items are completely visible in the drop-down list.

A-3: Setting date and list validation rules

Here's how	Here's why
1 Select C5:C20	You'll create a validation rule to ensure that the date of hire entered is on or before today's date.
Click **Data Validation**	To open the Data Validation dialog box.
2 Click the **Settings** tab	
3 From the Allow list, select **Date**	
From the Data list, select **less than or equal to**	
In the End date box, enter **=TODAY()**	
	To specify the validation date as today's date.
Click **OK**	To set the validation.
4 In C5, enter tomorrow's date	(In mm/dd/yy format.) An error message appears.
Click **Retry**	Or press Enter.
Enter a valid date of hire	A date earlier than or equal to today's date.
5 Select D5:D20	You'll create a list of valid departments from which the user can choose.
Click **Data Validation**	The Settings tab is active.
From the Allow list, select **List**	
In the Source box, enter **Accounting, Customer Service, Human Resources, Marketing, National Sales**	
	To create the list of values for the column. If the list of values appeared in the worksheet, you could enter the range in the Source box.
Click **OK**	To set the validation rule. A drop-down arrow appears to the right of D5.

Validation criteria

Allow:

Date

Data:

less than or equal to

End date:

=TODAY()

Validation criteria

Allow:

List

Data:

between

Source:

e, Human Resources, Marketing, National Sales

☑ Ignore blank

☑ In-cell dropdown

6 In D5, click the drop-down arrow

Department

Accounting
Customer Service
Human Resources
Marketing
National Sales

To display the list you just created.

Select **Marketing**

7 Update and close the workbook

Topic B: Exploring database functions

Explanation

A *database* is an organized collection of related information. In a database, the rows of related data are called *records*, and the columns are called *fields*. The first row of a database contains the names of the fields.

You can summarize values that meet complex criteria by using database functions, such as DSUM, DCOUNT, and DAVERAGE. For example, you can use DCOUNT to find the total number of salespeople who joined the staff of a specific store in a certain year.

The structure of database functions

The syntax of a database function is:

```
Dfunction(database,field,criteria)
```

In this syntax, the arguments are:

- database — The range containing the list of related information. Each row is a record, and each column is a field. The first row of the database must contain labels for each field.

- field — The column to be used by the function. Here you can specify the column name, such as Emp_Id, or a number that represents the position of the column in the database.

- criteria — The range that contains the conditions a row must meet to be included in the calculation. The function considers only those database records that meet the specified conditions. The first row of the criteria range must include field names that correspond precisely to field names in the database.

  When you include more than one row in the criteria range, the new row is considered to be an "Or" condition. That is, rows will be included if they match the conditions in the first row or if they match conditions in subsequent rows. An Or condition will typically increase the number of matching rows.

The following examples are based on the database shown in Exhibit 4-2:

- DSUM(database, "Current year",A2:B3) returns the total sales of Annatto Seed in the East region for the current year.

- DCOUNT(database, "Current year",A2:C3) returns the number of stores in the East region where total sales of Annatto Seed were less than $50,000 for the current year.

- DSUM(database, "Current year",A2:A4) returns the total sales of Annatto Seed and Anise Seeds for the current year.

	A	B	C	D	E
1	Criteria				
2	Product	Region	Current year		
3	Annatto Seed	East	<50,000		
4	Anise Seeds	North			
5					
6	Average current year sales of Annatto Seed in East				$30,479.90
7	Total current year sales of Annatto Seed and Anise Seeds				$623,570.92
8	Number of East region stores where current year total sales of Annatto Seed is less than $50,000				4
9					
10					
11	Database				
12	Product	Region	Store code	Prior year	Current year
13	Annatto Seed	East	ES008		$24,181.04
14	Cinnamon	East	ES008	$87,970.00	$67,240.00
15	Anise Seeds	East	ES211	$11,312.31	$20,218.31
16	Annatto Seed	East	ES211	$58,842.00	$49,530.00
17	Cinnamon	East	ES211	$99,665.00	$31,705.00
18	Anise Seeds	East	ES367	$22,772.00	$57,510.00
19	Annatto Seed	East	ES367	$17,990.07	$18,157.57
20	Asafoetida Powder	East	ES367	$19,425.69	$23,273.19
21	Cinnamon	East	ES367	$27,517.00	$49,425.00
22	Anise Seeds	East	ES783		$13,451.00
23	Annatto Seed	East	ES783	$47,345.00	$30,051.00
24	Cinnamon	East	ES783	$15,540.77	$22,730.88

Exhibit 4-2: A database function worksheet

Do it!   **B-1: Examining the structure of database functions**

The files for this activity are in Student Data folder **Unit 4\Topic B**.

Here's how	Here's why
1 Open Product sales	
Save the workbook as **My product sales**	In the current topic folder.
2 Click the Database functions sheet	(If necessary.) You'll examine the structure of database functions. The blank cells in the Prior year column indicate that this product was not sold by the specific store last year.
Select the range named Database	(Select Database from the Name box.) The first row in the range contains unique text labels or field names that identify the data in the columns below them.
Select the range named Criteria	This range specifies the conditions for the database functions. The first row contains field names that must exactly match those in the database.
3 Select E6	
Observe the formula bar	*fx* =DAVERAGE(Database,"Current year",A2:B3)
	This function calculates the average sales of Annatto Seed in the East region for the current year. In this formula, "Database" is the name of the range that forms the database, "Current year" indicates the column to be used in the function, and "A2:B3" is the criteria range.
4 Select E7	
Observe the formula bar	*fx* =DSUM(Database,5,A2:A4)
	This function sums the sales of Annatto Seed and Anise Seeds for the current year. In this formula, "5" represents the column on which the function will perform the calculation. You can use the column number or column name as this argument.
5 Select E8	*fx* =DCOUNT(Database,"Current year",A2:C3)
	This function counts the number of stores whose total sales for the current year were less than $50,000 in the East region.

The DSUM and DAVERAGE functions

Explanation

You can use the DSUM function to add only those values in a database column that meet a specified criterion. For example, you could use DSUM to calculate the total sales for a store in a specific year or for one product in a certain region. The syntax of DSUM is:

```
DSUM(database,field,criteria)
```

You can use the DAVERAGE function to average the values, in a column of a list or database, that match conditions you specify. The syntax of DAVERAGE is:

```
DAVERAGE(database,field,criteria)
```

Do it!

B-2: Using the DSUM function

Here's how	Here's why
1 Click the DSUM sheet	
Select the range named Database	(If necessary.) This range forms the database.
Observe A1:B3	<table><tr><th></th><th>A</th><th>B</th></tr><tr><td>1</td><td>Product</td><td>Quality grade</td></tr><tr><td>2</td><td>Annatto Seed</td><td>A</td></tr><tr><td>3</td><td>Anise Seeds</td><td>A</td></tr></table>
	This is the criteria range that you will use in the first DSUM function.
2 Select D5	You'll calculate the total sales of Annatto Seed and Anise Seeds of grade A quality.
Type **=DSUM(Database,**	In this formula, "Database" is the name of the range that represents the database.
Type **"Sales",**	This indicates the column on which the function will perform the calculation.
Type **A1:B3)**	"A1:B3" specifies the criteria range.
Press (← ENTER)	The function displays $57,850.35, which is the total sales figure for Annatto Seed and Anise Seeds of grade A quality.
3 Observe D1:F2	<table><tr><th>D</th><th>E</th><th>F</th></tr><tr><td>Product</td><td>Quality grade</td><td>Quality grade</td></tr><tr><td>Annatto Seed</td><td>>A</td><td><E</td></tr></table>
	This criteria range specifies rows in which the grade is both "greater than" A and "less than" E. For letters, this means that the grade characters fall between A and E, in alphabetical order.

4 Select D6	(If necessary.) You'll sum the values in the Sales column for the Annatto Seed records where the quality grades are B, C, and D.
Type **=DSUM(Database,"Sales",**	
Type **D1:F2)**	To specify the criteria range.
Press ⏎ ENTER	The function displays $139,843.45, which is the total sales figure for Annatto Seed of grades B, C, and D.
5 Update and close the workbook	

Unit summary: Advanced data management

Topic A

In this topic, you learned that **data validation** ensures the entry of valid information in a worksheet. You specified a set of rules to validate data. You also specified input messages and error messages to be displayed to prompt the user to enter correct data.

Topic B

In this topic, you learned about **database functions**, such as DSUM, DAVERAGE, and DCOUNT. You learned that database functions are used to summarize data according to specified criteria. You also used the **DSUM** function to add values that meet complex criteria.

Independent practice activity

In this activity, you'll perform calculations by using several Excel functions. You'll also create data validation rules and use the DCOUNT function.

The files for this activity are in Student Data folder **Unit 4\Unit summary**.

1 Open Sales figures, and ensure that the Data validation worksheet is active.

2 Save the workbook as **My sales figures**.

3 Create a data validation rule to accept only those Store codes with lengths between four and six characters and residing in the range A5:A24. (*Hint:* Data Validation is in the Data Tools group on the Data tab.)

4 For the range B5:B24, create a list of regions from which users can choose. The list should contain **East**, **North**, **South**, and **West**. Also, ensure that a proper error message appears when the user enters an invalid region.

5 Create a data validation rule to ensure that the range C5:C24 accepts only whole numbers greater than zero.

6 Test your new data validation rules. Make any necessary adjustments.

7 Click the Database functions worksheet. In H5, enter a database function that counts the number of salespeople whose total sales were greater than $10,000 and whose sales in quarter 3 were greater than $3,000. (*Hint:* Use the DCOUNT function. Compare your worksheet to Exhibit 4-3. If you need help with the formula, scroll down to A100.)

8 Update and close the workbook.

	A	B	C	D	E	F	G	H
1	Criteria							
2	Total sales	Qtr3						
3	>10000	>3000						
4								
5	Number of salespeople whose total sales is greater than $10,000 and whose							
6	sales in quarter 3 are greater than $3,000							4
7								
8	Database							
9	Salesperson	Qtr1	Qtr2	Qtr3	Qtr4	Total sales		
10	Bill MacArthur	$ 2,500	$ 2,750	$ 3,500	$ 3,700	$ 12,450		
11	Jamie Morrison	$ 3,560	$ 3,000	$ 1,700	$ 2,000	$ 10,260		
12	Maureen O'Connor	$ 4,500	$ 4,000	$ 3,500	$ 3,700	$ 15,700		
13	Rebecca Austin	$ 3,250	$ 2,725	$ 3,000	$ 3,250	$ 12,225		
14	Paul Anderson	$ 2,520	$ 2,000	$ 2,500	$ 2,700	$ 9,720		
15	Cynthia Roberts	$ 1,500	$ 1,700	$ 1,800	$ 2,000	$ 7,000		
16	Rita Greg	$ 4,590	$ 4,050	$ 4,500	$ 3,700	$ 16,840		
17	Trevor Johnson	$ 3,660	$ 3,200	$ 3,000	$ 2,250	$ 12,110		
18	Kevin Meyers	$ 1,790	$ 1,800	$ 2,000	$ 2,200	$ 7,790		
19	Adam Long	$ 1,700	$ 1,950	$ 2,500	$ 2,750	$ 8,900		
20	Kendra James	$ 1,650	$ 2,000	$ 1,500	$ 1,750	$ 6,900		
21	Michael Lee	$ 2,050	$ 2,500	$ 2,800	$ 3,200	$ 10,550		
22	Sandra Lawrence	$ 3,425	$ 3,750	$ 4,000	$ 3,120	$ 14,295		
23	Mary Smith	$ 4,540	$ 2,700	$ 3,000	$ 3,200	$ 13,440		
24	Annie Philips	$ 1,200	$ 1,700	$ 1,800	$ 2,000	$ 6,700		

Exhibit 4-3: The Database functions worksheet after Step 7

Review questions

1 What's the purpose of validating data?

2 List the steps you would use to set data validation rules.

3 What is the syntax of the DSUM function?

Unit 5

Exporting and importing

Complete this unit, and you'll know how to:

A Export data from Excel to a text file, and import data from a text file into an Excel workbook.

B Import XML data into a workbook, and export data from a workbook to an XML data file.

C Use Microsoft Query and the Web query feature to import data from external databases.

Topic A: Exporting and importing text files

You can share information between Excel and other programs in a number of ways, including by using linked objects and copied data. Another way to share data is to export it from Excel to another format or to import data from another format into Excel. Excel can import from and export to files in several formats, including text files.

Using the Save As command to export data

You can use the Save As command to save an Excel workbook in a file format associated with the program in which you want to use the data. However, when you save an Excel workbook in a different file format, it might not retain its original formatting.

The following table describes some formats commonly used to export Excel data.

File format	Description
Text (tab delimited)	• Saves text and values as they appear in the worksheet • Saves formulas as text • Uses tab characters to separate columns of data • Uses paragraph marks to separate rows • Loses any formatting, graphics, and objects in the worksheet • Can be a useful way to fix a corrupted file
XML Paper Specification (XPS)	• Preserves formatting and graphics • Enables file sharing • Prevents data from being changed • XPS View is installed by default
Portable Document Format (PDF)	• Preserves formatting and graphics • Enables file sharing • Provides a standard format when using commercial printers • Abode Reader is freely available for download
Open Document Spreadsheet (ODS)	• Maintains some formatting, but not all • Opens in spreadsheet applications such as Google Docs

Do it!

A-1:   Exporting Excel data to a text file

The files for this activity are in Student Data folder **Unit 5\Topic A**.

Here's how	Here's why
1 Open Regional sales	
2 Open the Save As dialog box	The File name box contains "Regional sales."
Edit the File name box to read **My regional sales**	
From the Save as type list, select **Text (Tab delimited)**	File name: My regional sales Save as type: Text (Tab delimited)
	This option will save the active sheet as a tab-delimited text file.
Click **Save**	To save the active sheet as a text file. A message appears, stating that Excel will not save those features that are not compatible with the Text (Tab delimited) file format.
Click **Yes**	To keep the tab-delimited format.
3 Click **Start**	
Choose **All Programs, Accessories, Notepad**	To open the Notepad program.
Open the My regional sales text file	(From the current topic folder.) The data from the Regional sales worksheet appears in the text file. All of the sales figures that contain commas appear in double quotation marks.
4 Switch to Excel	If necessary.
5 Close the workbook	You don't need to save changes.

Importing data

Explanation

By using the Open command in Excel, you can open a file created in a program other than Excel. After importing the data, you can save the file either in its original format or as an Excel workbook.

To import a file into an Excel workbook, you open the Open dialog box, specify the type of file you want to import, select the file, and click Open.

If you're importing a text file, Excel displays the Text Import Wizard, shown in Exhibit 5-1. The wizard guides you through the process of converting the text data into an Excel worksheet. As necessary, you can specify *delimiters* (the characters that determine when a new column should begin) and formatting for specific columns. After importing, you can separate text into columns, if necessary, by clicking Text to Columns in the Data Tools group on the Data tab.

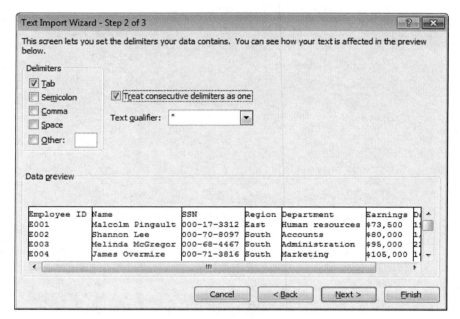

Exhibit 5-1: Step 2 of the Text Import Wizard

Do it!

A-2: Importing data from a text file into a workbook

The files for this activity are in Student Data folder **Unit 5\Topic A**.

Here's how	Here's why
1 Switch to Notepad	Click the Notepad taskbar button. The text file "My regional sales" is still open.
Open the Employee List text file	You'll import data from this text file into Excel. This file contains details for employees, with columns separated by tab characters.
Observe the date format in the last column	The person who entered this data used the European day/month/year format, not the American month/day/year format.
2 Close Notepad	
3 Switch to Excel	If necessary.
4 Display the Open dialog box	
In the Address bar, select the current topic folder	If necessary.
5 Select **Text Files**	All Excel Files ▼ All Files All Excel Files Excel Files All Web Pages XML Files Text Files All Data Sources To display only the text files in the current topic folder.
Select **Employee list**	To select the file you want to import.
6 Click **Open**	To open Step 1 of the Text Import Wizard. Under Original data type, Delimited is selected. The "Start import at row" box displays "1."
Click **Next**	In Step 2 of the Text Import Wizard, you can set the delimiter and see a preview of the data. Here, Tab is the default delimiter.
Under Data preview, observe the box	This box shows you how the data will look in Excel. Data in a few columns is misaligned with the headings because of the consecutive tabs.
Check **Treat consecutive delimiters as one**	To remove the blank columns, as shown in Exhibit 5-1.

7	Click **Next**	In Step 3 of the Text Import Wizard, you can specify the data format for each column.
8	Select the last column	(Scroll to the right as necessary.) You must indicate that the values are currently in DMY (day/month/year) format for Excel to be able to change the formatting to the American MDY format.
	Under Column data format, select **Date** From the Date format list, select **DMY**	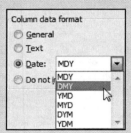
9	Click **Finish**	To close the Text Import Wizard.

	A	B	C	D	E	F	G
1	Employee	Name	SSN	Region	Departme	Earnings	Date of Hire
2	E001	Malcolm F	000-17-33!	East	Human re	$73,500	########
3	E002	Shannon L	000-70-80!	South	Accounts	$80,000	2/1/2002
4	E003	Melinda N	000-68-44!	South	Administr	$95,000	########
5	E004	James Ov	000-71-38!	South	Marketing	$105,000	########
6	E005	Roger Wil	000-98-75!	East	Customer	$90,000	########
7	E005	Roger Wil	000-98-75!	East	Customer	$90,000	########
8	E006	Annie Phi	000-85-85!	West	Human re	$60,000	########
9	E007	Melissa Ja	000-78-89!	East	Accounts	$87,000	########
10	E008	Mary Smit	000-58-95!	North	Administr	$104,000	5/7/2000
11	E009	Rita Greg	000-07-57!	East	Sales	$380,050	########
12	E010	Trevor Jot	000-31-33!	North	Sales	$93,000	########
13	E011	Paul Ande	000-76-88!	East	Human re	$180,000	4/1/1998
14	E012	Rebecca A	000-20-99!	South	Marketing	$100,000	9/6/1999

		The worksheet shows the data from the text file. Some columns are too narrow to display all of the data.
10	Select columns A through G	Drag through the column headings.
	Double-click the dividing line between any two selected column headings	To automatically fit the width to the column contents.
11	Observe the Date of Hire column data	

G
Date of Hire
4/19/2001
2/1/2002
7/22/1999
6/14/1997
10/2/1996
10/2/1996

Excel converted the dates to the MDY format.

12	Open the Save As dialog box	The File name box contains "Employee list," and the Save as type list displays "Text (Tab delimited)."
	From the Save as type list, select **Excel Workbook**	(You might have to scroll up the list.) To save the data in an Excel workbook.
	Edit the File name box to read **My employee list**	
13	Click **Save**	

Converting text to columns

Explanation

You can use the Text to Columns feature to divide text fields into two or more columns. This process works much like importing data from external text files. For instance, if you have one field for names, you can split this field into first-name and last-name columns. To do so, select the text field you want to convert and click Text to Columns on the Data tab. Follow the instructions in the Convert Text to Columns Wizard, shown in Exhibit 5-2.

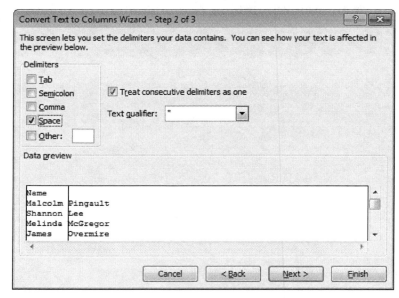

Exhibit 5-2: Step 2 of the Convert Text to Columns Wizard

Do it!   ## A-3:   Converting text to columns

Here's how	Here's why
1 Insert a column after column B	(Select column C, right-click it, and choose Insert.) To make room for the new column for storing last names.
2 Select column B	This is the Name column in the data you just imported from a text file.
3 On the Data tab, in the Data Tools group, click **Text to Columns**	

Text to Columns

To start the Convert Text to Columns Wizard. This is like a mini version of the Text Import Wizard.

Here's how	Here's why
4 Click **Next**	
5 Under Delimiters, clear **Tab** and check **Space**	As shown in Exhibit 5-2.
Check **Treat consecutive delimiters as one**	If necessary.
Click **Next**	To proceed to the last step in the wizard.
6 Verify that **General** is selected as the column data format	Note that the column heading Name appears in the first-name column. You'll change the heading after the conversion.
7 Click **Finish**	To close the wizard and return to the table. First and last names are now split into two columns. If you hadn't inserted a new column, Excel would have asked if you wanted to replace the existing data.
8 Edit B1 to read **First Name**	
9 In C1, enter **Last Name**	
10 Adjust column widths as necessary	Select columns B and C and then double-click the divider between them.
11 Update the workbook	

Removing duplicates

Explanation

Sometimes, especially when you import data from one or more external sources, you can end up with duplicate records. Using the Remove Duplicates dialog box, shown in Exhibit 5-3, you can remove duplicate records based on values in one or more fields. For instance, if you imported customer data from several sources because you want to compile e-mail addresses for a mailing, you can remove duplicates based on the E-mail field.

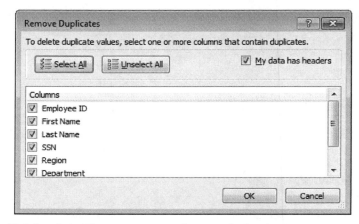

Exhibit 5-3: The Remove Duplicates dialog box

Do it!

A-4: Removing duplicate records

Here's how	Here's why
1 Observe employee numbers E005, E015, and E019	The table has duplicate records.
2 Select the table	

	A	B
1	Employee ID	First Name
2	E001	Malcolm

Click the selector in the upper-left corner, as shown.

Here's how	Here's why
3 On the Data tab, in the Data Tools group, click **Remove Duplicates**	

Remove Duplicates

To open the Remove Duplicates dialog box.

Here's how	Here's why
4 Click **Unselect All**	You need to search only one column.
5 Check **SSN**	

Columns
- [ ] Employee ID
- [ ] First Name
- [ ] Last Name
- [x] SSN
- [ ] Region
- [ ] Department

You'll search for duplicates based on the Social Security number, which should be a unique identifier.

Here's how	Here's why
6 Click **OK**	To close the Remove Duplicates dialog box. A message box informs you that three duplicates were found and removed.
Click **OK**	To close the message box.
7 Update and close the workbook	

Topic B: Exporting and importing XML data

This topic covers the following Microsoft Office Specialist objectives for exam 77-888: Excel Expert 2010.

#	Objective
1.1	**Apply workbook settings, properties, and data options**
	1.1.3 Import and export XML data

The XML Source task pane

Explanation

Extensible Markup Language (XML) is a set of rules for structuring and designing data formats that are exchanged between applications. You can import data from an XML file into an Excel workbook. You can also export data from a workbook to an XML file. To import or export XML data, you use the XML Source pane to map the workbook to a user-defined XML schema (.xsd file).

The XML Source task pane helps you map an Excel workbook to an XML schema. This pane also provides options for importing and exporting XML data. You can also refresh the imported data to reflect the latest changes in the source data.

To map a workbook to a user-defined XML schema:

1   Click the Developer tab. If it's not visible, enable it:

   a   Open the Excel Options dialog box.

   b   In the left pane, select Customize Ribbon. In the right pane, under Main Tabs, check Developer. Click OK.

2   On the Developer tab, in the XML group, click Source to display the XML Source pane.

3   In the pane, click XML Maps to open the XML Maps dialog box.

4   Click Add to open the Select XML Source dialog box. Browse to locate the .xsd file, and click Open.

5   In the Multiple Roots dialog box that appears, select the .xsd file and click OK. The added map appears in the XML Maps dialog box, shown in Exhibit 5-4.

6   Click OK to close the XML Maps dialog box. The file and the elements in it appear in the XML Source pane, shown in Exhibit 5-5.

7   To map the XML schema to the workbook, drag the elements from the pane to the corresponding cells in the workbook. The mapped areas appear in blue with nonprintable borders.

Exhibit 5-4: The XML Maps dialog box

Exhibit 5-5: The XML Source pane

Defining XML options

The XML Source pane also provides options to display XML data in a worksheet in different formats. Click the Options button in the pane and choose the option you want. The options are:

- **Preview Data in Task Pane** — Displays data in the XML Source pane when you import XML data.

- **Hide Help Text in the Task Pane** — Hides the help text that appears below the list of schema elements in the XML Source pane.

- **Automatically Merge Elements When Mapping** — Expands an XML List automatically when you drag an element from the XML Source pane to a cell that is outside the XML List but adjacent to it.

- **My Data Has Headings** — Uses existing data as column headings when you create XML maps.

Do it!

B-1: Using the XML Source pane

The files for this activity are in Student Data folder **Unit 5\Topic B**.

Here's how	Here's why
1 Open Employee details	(You might need to select Excel Files from the Files of type list in the Open dialog box.) You'll create an XML map for this workbook.
Save the workbook as **My employee details**	In the current topic folder.
2 Click the **Developer** tab	If the Developer tab does not appear, open the Excel Options dialog box, click Customize Ribbon, check Developer (under Main Tabs), and click OK.
3 In the XML group, click **Source**	To display the XML Source pane.
4 Click **XML Maps**	(In the XML Source pane.) To open the XML Maps dialog box.
Click **Add**	To open the Select XML Source dialog box.
5 Navigate to the current topic folder	
Select **EmployeeRecord.xsd**	This is the file containing the XML schema.
Click **Open**	

The Multiple Roots dialog box opens with EmployeeRecord selected.

6 Click **OK**	A message box appears, asking if you want to continue adding this schema to your workbook.
Click **Yes**	Your XML Maps dialog box should match Exhibit 5-4.
7 Click **OK**	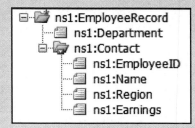 To close the XML Maps dialog box. You can see the .xsd file, along with its elements, in the XML Source pane.
8 In the XML Source pane, press and hold the mouse button while pointing to **ns1:Department**	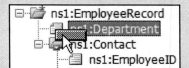 The solid bar represents the Department element.
9 Drag the **ns1:Department** icon to the worksheet, as shown	 To map the Department element in the XML schema to the worksheet.
Deselect A8	(Click anywhere in the worksheet.) Now the cell has a blue border, indicating that the cell is mapped to an XML schema.
10 Drag **ns1:EmployeeID** to A11	
Drag **ns1:Name** to B11	
Drag **ns1:Region** to C11	
Drag **ns1:Earnings** to D11	
11 Select E11	To deselect the mapped cells.
12 Update the workbook	

Importing XML data into a workbook

Explanation

After creating an XML map, you can import data in an XML format into a workbook.

To import XML data:

1 Click the Developer tab.

2 In the XML group, click Import to open the Import XML dialog box.

3 Select the XML file containing the data. You can use the Address bar to locate the file, if necessary.

4 Click Import. The values in the XML file appear in the corresponding cells in the workbook, as shown in Exhibit 5-6.

7	Department			
8	Human resources			
9				
10	EmployeeID ▼	Name ▼	Region ▼	Earnings ▼
11	E001	Malcolm Pingault	East	$73,500
12	E006	Annie Philips	West	$60,000
13	E011	Paul Anderson	East	$180,000
14	E019	Jamie Morrison	East	$62,000

Exhibit 5-6: XML data imported into a workbook

Do it!

B-2: Importing XML data into a workbook

The files for this activity are in Student Data folder **Unit 5\Topic B**.

Here's how	Here's why
1 In the XML group, click **Import**	(On the Developer tab.) To open the Import XML dialog box.
2 Select **EmployeeInfo**	(From the current topic folder.) This XML file contains values for fields such as Department, EmployeeID, Name, Region, and Earnings in the workbook.
3 Click **Import**	You'll see that the values corresponding to Department, EmployeeID, Name, Region, and Earnings appear in the corresponding cells, as shown in Exhibit 5-6. The Trace Error button appears if you select a value in the Earnings column, because those values are stored as text instead of numbers. We won't worry about this now, though.
4 Update and close the workbook	

Exporting data to XML files

Explanation   You can modify the data in a workbook and then export it in XML format so that it can be used by other applications. You can also add or delete records in the workbook.

For you to export data, the workbook should contain a valid XML map. Excel will validate the worksheet data against this map before exporting. To export the workbook data, click Export in the XML group on the Developer tab.

Do it!   ### B-3:   Exporting data from a workbook to an XML data file

The files for this activity are in Student Data folder **Unit 5\Topic B**.

Here's how	Here's why
1 Open Export	
2 Display the XML Source pane	(Click XML Source on the Developer tab, if necessary.) The workbook is mapped to EmployeeRecord.
3 Save the workbook as **My export**	In the current topic folder.
4 In A21, enter **E038**	To enter the employee ID for someone who has joined the Accounting department.
In B21, enter **David Ford**	
5 In C21, enter **South**	
6 Copy the value in D17	
Paste it in D21	
7 Right-click row heading **16**	(The number 16 at the left end of that row.) This row contains the record for an employee who has left the Accounting department.
Choose **Delete**	To delete the record.
8 Update the workbook	
9 Click the **Developer** tab	If necessary.
10 In the XML group, click **Export**	To open the Export XML dialog box.
In the Address bar, select the current topic folder	If necessary.
In the File name box, enter **My export**	
11 Click **Export**	To export the workbook as an XML file.

Deleting XML maps

Explanation

After importing or exporting data, you no longer need to map the workbook to an XML schema. Therefore, you can delete the XML maps. When you delete a map, the data in the workbook remains.

To delete an XML map:

1 In the XML Source pane, click XML Maps to open the XML Maps dialog box.
2 Select the XML map you want to delete.
3 Click Delete. A message box appears, warning that you'll no longer be able to import or export XML data by using the XML map. Click OK.
4 Click OK.

Do it!

B-4: Deleting an XML map

Here's how	Here's why
1 In the XML Source pane, click **XML Maps**	To open the XML Maps dialog box.
2 In the "XML maps in this workbook" list, select the XML map	

XML maps in this workbook:

Name	Root	Namespace
EmployeeRecord_Map	EmployeeRecord	http://MyEmployeeData/EmployeeRecord.xsd

Click **Delete**	A message warns you that you'll no longer be able to import or export XML data with this XML map.
Click **OK**	To delete the XML map and close the message box. The XML Maps dialog box no longer displays the XML map.
3 Click **OK**	To close the XML Maps dialog box.
4 Observe the workbook	The data in the workbook remains intact.
5 Update and close the workbook	

Topic C: Getting external data

This topic covers the following Microsoft Office Specialist objectives for exam 77-888: Excel Expert 2010.

#	Objective
2.4	**Apply functions in formulas**
	2.4.8 Cube functions
3.5	**Demonstrate how to use the slicer**
	3.5.1 Choose data sets from external data connections

Microsoft Query

Explanation

With Microsoft Query, you can retrieve data from external databases, such as those in Microsoft Access. You can use the Web query feature to retrieve data from the Web.

You can use Microsoft Query to retrieve data that meets certain conditions in one or more tables of a database. For example, from an Employee table, you can retrieve the records of all people who work in the Marketing department.

To retrieve data by using Microsoft Query:

1 Click the Data tab.

2 In the Get External Data group, click From Other Sources and choose From Microsoft Query to start the Microsoft Query program and to open the Choose Data Source dialog box, shown in Exhibit 5-7.

3 On the Databases tab, select <New Data Source> and click OK to open the Create New Data Source dialog box. Specify the name of the data source and select a driver for the database. Click Connect to open the ODBC Microsoft Access Setup dialog box.

4 Under Database, click Select to open the Select Database dialog box. Select the source database, and then return to the Choose Data Source dialog box.

5 Select the data source, and click OK to open the Choose Columns page of the Query Wizard. Add the tables and fields you want to include in your result set. Click Next to open the Filter Data page of the Query Wizard.

6 Specify the conditions you want the data to meet. Click Next to open the Sort Order page of the Query Wizard.

7 Specify the sort order for the data. Click Next to open the Finish page of the Query Wizard.

8 Select Return Data to Microsoft Office Excel. Click Finish to close the wizard and to open the Import Data dialog box.

9 Specify whether you want to place the data in the existing worksheet or in a new worksheet.

10 Click OK to import the data.

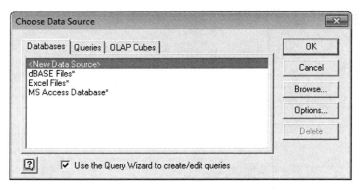

Exhibit 5-7: The Choose Data Source dialog box

Do it!

C-1: Getting external data from Microsoft Query

The files for this activity are in Student Data folder **Unit 5\Topic C**.

Here's how	Here's why
1 Open Query	(You might need to select Excel Files from the Files of type list in the Open dialog box.) This workbook contains two worksheets. QueryDb is the active sheet. You'll use the Microsoft Query program to retrieve data from an Access database and place it in this worksheet.
2 Save the workbook as **My query**	In the current topic folder.
3 Click the **Data** tab	
4 In the Get External Data group, click **From Other Sources**	**From SQL Server** — Create a connection to a SQL Server table. Import data into Excel as a Table or PivotTable report. **From Analysis Services** — Create a connection to a SQL Server Analysis Services cube. Import data into Excel as a Table or PivotTable report. **From XML Data Import** — Open or map a XML file into Excel. **From Data Connection Wizard** — Import data for an unlisted format by using the Data Connection Wizard and OLEDB. **From Microsoft Query** — Import data for an unlisted format by using the Microsoft Query Wizard and ODBC.
	To display a list of sources.
Choose **From Microsoft Query**	To open the Choose Data Source dialog box. By default, the Databases tab is active. You can either select an existing data source or create a new one.

5 Verify that **<New Data Source>** is selected

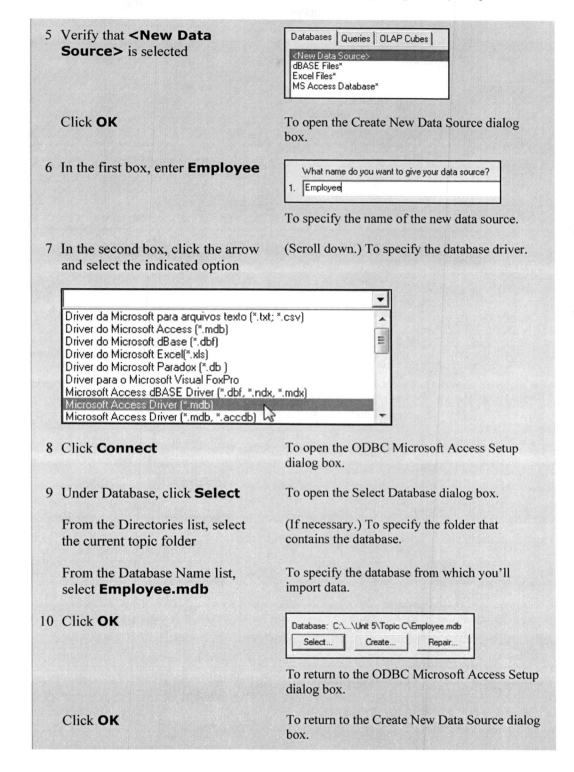

Click **OK**   To open the Create New Data Source dialog box.

6 In the first box, enter **Employee**

To specify the name of the new data source.

7 In the second box, click the arrow and select the indicated option   (Scroll down.) To specify the database driver.

8 Click **Connect**   To open the ODBC Microsoft Access Setup dialog box.

9 Under Database, click **Select**   To open the Select Database dialog box.

From the Directories list, select the current topic folder   (If necessary.) To specify the folder that contains the database.

From the Database Name list, select **Employee.mdb**   To specify the database from which you'll import data.

10 Click **OK**

To return to the ODBC Microsoft Access Setup dialog box.

Click **OK**   To return to the Create New Data Source dialog box.

11 From the last list, select **Employees**

> Select a default table for your data source
> 4.
>
> Departments
> Employees
> Query1
> Sales employees
> Sales payroll

To specify which of the tables in the Employee database should act as the default for building queries.

12 Click **OK**

> Databases | Queries | OLAP Cubes
>
> <New Data Source>
> dBASE Files*
> Employee
> Excel Files*
> MS Access Database*

To return to the Choose Data Source dialog box. The Employee data source has been added to the list and is selected.

13 Click **OK**

To close the Choose Data Source dialog box and open the Choose Columns page of the Query Wizard. In the "Available tables and columns" list, Employees is selected.

Click [>]

> Columns in your query:
>
> Ecode
> Lname
> Fname
> Region
> Dept code

To include all columns of the Employees table in the query. The columns of the Employees table now appear in the "Columns in your query" list.

14 Click **Next**

To open the Filter Data page of the Query Wizard. The group box under "Only include rows where" is not available and has no name.

From the Column to filter list, select **Dept code**

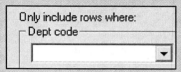

The group box under "Only include rows where" is now available and is named "Dept code." The first list under Dept code is also available.

From the first list under Dept code, select **equals**

To specify the comparison operator for the query.

From the second list under Dept code, select **MKTG**

To specify that the result of this query includes only those rows where the Dept code is MKTG.

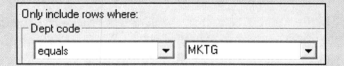

15 Click **Next**

To open the Sort Order page of the Query Wizard.

From the Sort by list, select **Region**

This will sort data by Region. By default, Ascending is selected.

16 Click **Next**

To open the Finish page of the Query Wizard. By default, Return Data to Microsoft Office Excel is selected.

17 Click **Finish**

The Import Data dialog box appears, prompting you to specify the destination for the data. Cell A1 in the existing worksheet is selected by default.

18 Click **OK**

	A	B	C	D	E
1	Ecode	Lname	Fname	Region	Dept code
2	E-09	Greg	Rita	East	MKTG
3	E-12	Austin	Rebecca	North	MKTG
4	E-10	Johnson	Trevor	South	MKTG
5	E-11	Anderson	Paul	West	MKTG

The records of all employees in the Marketing department appear in the worksheet.

19 Update the workbook

The Web query feature

Explanation

If you want to analyze data on the Web, such as online currency rates or stock quotes, you can create a Web query. When you run a Web query, Excel retrieves data that has been marked up with Hypertext Markup Language (HTML) or Extensible Markup Language (XML).

HTML and XML

The focus of HTML, which consists primarily of predefined tags, is the appearance of the content in a browser window. XML, on the other hand, focuses on the content and not on its appearance. There are no predefined tags in XML; instead, you create your own tags to give your data meaning and structure. Both markup languages are related to a parent language, SGML (Standard Generalized Markup Language), which provides rules for marking up documents and data.

Retrieving data from the Web

To retrieve data from a Web page:

1 Click the Data tab. Then, in the Get External Data group, click From Web to open the New Web Query dialog box.

2 In the Address box, enter the address of the Web page from which you want to retrieve data, as shown in Exhibit 5-8.

3 Click the arrow next to the table you want to select.

4 Click Options to open the Web Query Options dialog box. Select the format in which you want the data to be displayed. Click OK.

5 Click Import to open the Import Data dialog box. Specify whether you want the data to be placed in an existing worksheet or a new worksheet. Click OK.

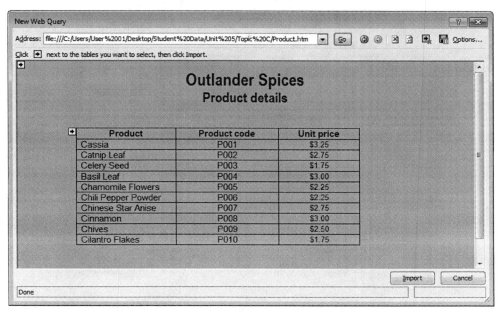

Exhibit 5-8: The New Web Query dialog box

Do it!

C-2: Using a Web query to get data from the Web

The files for this activity are in Student Data folder **Unit 5\Topic C**.

Here's how	Here's why
1 Click the WebQ sheet	You'll use the Web query program to retrieve data from a Web page.
Click the **Data** tab	If necessary.
2 In the Get External Data group, click **From Web**	To open the New Web Query dialog box.
3 In the Address box, enter **C:\Users*User name*\Desktop\Student Data\Unit 5\Topic C\Product.htm**	
	(Use the current unit number and topic letter.) This is the address of the Web page that contains the relevant data.
Click **Go**	The preview of the Web page appears in the dialog box.
4 Click the arrow to the left of the table, as shown	To import data from the table on the Web page.
5 Click **Options**, as shown	To open the Web Query Options dialog box.
Under Formatting, select **Full HTML formatting**	To retain the current formatting of the table.
Click **OK**	
6 Click **Import**	To open the Import Data dialog box. By default, the Existing worksheet option is selected.
Click **OK**	

	A	B	C
1	Product	Product code	Unit price
2	Cassia	P001	$3.25
3	Catnip Leaf	P002	$2.75
4	Celery Seed	P003	$1.75
5	Basil Leaf	P004	$3.00
6	Chamomile Flowers	P005	$2.25
7	Chili Pepper Powder	P006	$2.25
8	Chinese Star Anise	P007	$2.75
9	Cinnamon	P008	$3.00
10	Chives	P009	$2.50
11	Cilantro Flakes	P010	$1.75

The data from the table on the Web page appears in the worksheet.

7 Update and close the workbook

OLAP data and cube functions

Explanation

Another type of external data source is known as an *Online Analytical Processing* (OLAP) database. As its name suggests, this database is stored on a SQL Server running Analysis Service and is accessed through your network connection.

OLAP databases are different from relational databases, such as Microsoft Access. In a relational database, records are arranged in tables, and the tables relate to each other. As tables are added, the relationships can get complicated and hard to understand. In an OLAP database, the relationships and hierarchies are stored in OLAP cubes. Cubes provide a multi-dimensional way to look at data. When OLAP data is imported into Excel, it is brought into the worksheet as a PivotTable.

OLAP cube structure

The components of an OLAP cube are dimensions, hierarchies, levels, members, and measures. *Drilling down* is the act of analyzing the data down to the greatest level of detail. Exhibit 5-10 illustrates this process, using our sample data and the Time dimension. With these in mind, let's examine the components of a sample OLAP cube:

- **Dimensions** — The major classifications of data. For example, our cube contains the dimensions shown in Exhibit 5-9.
- **Hierarchies** — Levels within a dimension that are used to pivot and analyze multiple components at once. In Exhibit 5-10, our example Time dimension contains a Calendar Year and a Fiscal Year.
- **Levels** — Groups of data that can be analyzed individually like data fields, such as Month or Quarter.
- **Members** — The individual data items within each level, such as the specific month (January, February, March, and so on).
- **Measures** — The actual data values, such as the sales dollars, sales count, and profit. *Slicing* the measures is the act of creating a query based on any combination of measures. In Excel 2010, you can use slicers to filter cube data just as you would use them to filter standard PivotTable data.

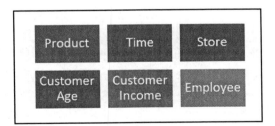

Exhibit 5-9: A sample set of cube dimensions

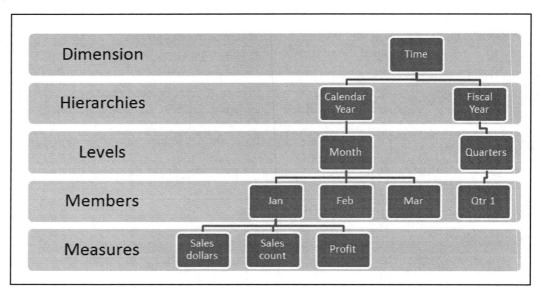

Exhibit 5-10: A sample Time dimension

Cube functions in Excel

Excel 2010 provides built-in cube functions to help you analyze the OLAP cube data. Creating and setting up an OLAP cube will require assistance from your organization's IT experts and network administrators.

The syntax of cube functions is:

```
=CUBE_FUNCTION (connection, member_expression, [caption])
```

The arguments are:

- `connection` — A text string identifying the name of the connection to the cube. Suppose that the connection to our example cube database is named GlobalSales. The first argument in any cube function would be "GlobalSales."
- `member_expression` — A text string, cell range, or array constant that points to a unique member in the cube.
- `caption` — Text to be displayed as a descriptive caption (optional).

Excel 2010 provides the following seven cube functions, which can be used to extract and analyze cubes:

- CUBEVALUE defines a single or combined value from the cube.
- CUBESET defines a calculated set of members.
- CUBESETCOUNT defines the number of items in a set.
- CUBEKPIMEMBER defines a *key performance indicator* (KPI) property and displays the KPI name in the cell. A KPI is a quantifiable measurement that is used to monitor a company's performance.
- CUBEMEMBER defines a member from the cube.
- CUBERANKEDMEMBER defines the nth, or ranked, member in a set. For example, you can use this function to return the top ten sales amounts.
- CUBEMEMBERPROPERTY defines the value of a member property from the cube.

Importing OLAP cube data into an Excel PivotTable

1 On the Data tab, in the Get External Data group, click From Other Sources.

2 In the Data Connection Wizard, enter the server name, user name, and password. Click Next.

3 From the list of databases, select the database.

4 Check "Connect to a specific cube or table," if necessary, and select the table.

5 Click Finish.

6 In the Import Data dialog box, select PivotTable Report. You can select "Only Create Connection" if you want to store the connection for reference later.

7 Click OK. The OLAP data is imported as a PivotTable into the Excel workbook.

Now, you can create the PivotTable using the cube data by dragging the desired cube components into the appropriate row and column areas. For more information about PivotTables and cube data, check out online help at Office.com.

Creating an Offline OLAP cube

If you want to work with your OLAP cube data when you are disconnected from the SQL Server, you can save the data as an offline cube file, with the file extension .cub. Keep in mind that the offline data is a snapshot of the data at a specific time.

1 Select any cell in the PivotTable.

2 On the PivotTable Tools | Options tab, click OLAP Tools and choose Offline OLAP.

3 In the Offline OLAP Settings dialog box, click the Create Offline Data File button to launch the Create Cube File Wizard.

4 Read the first step screen to learn about the cube wizard. Click Next.

5 In step 2 of the wizard, select the dimensions and levels to be included in the cube file. Click Next.

6 In step 3 of the wizard, select the items from each level to be included in the cube file. Click Next.

7 In step 4 of the wizard, specify the path and file name for the offline cube file. Click Finish.

Once you reconnect to the network, you can refresh the data and its corresponding PivotTable. In Excel 2010, the new *write-back* feature enables you to update the OLAP cube with new values.

Do it!   **C-3:**   **Discussing cube functions**

Questions and answers

1   What is OLAP?

2   How does an OLAP cube database differ from a relational database?

3   What is the highest level of categorization in a cube?

    A   Measure

    B   Hierarchy

    C   Members

    D   Dimension

4   What is the syntax for cube functions?

5   What's the advantage of creating an offline cube file?

Unit summary: Exporting and importing

Topic A   In this topic, you **exported data** from Excel to a text file. You **imported data** from a text file into an Excel workbook. You also separated the imported data into columns.

Topic B   In this topic, you used the **XML Source pane** to create an **XML map** for a workbook. You also used the XML Source pane to import XML data into an Excel workbook and to export data from a workbook to an XML file. In addition, you deleted an XML map.

Topic C   In this topic, you used **Microsoft Query** to retrieve data from an Access database. You also learned how to use the **Web query** feature to retrieve data from Web pages in HTML or XML format. Finally, you discussed OLAP cubes and **cube functions**.

Independent practice activity

In this activity, you'll export data from a worksheet to a text file. You'll create an XML map for a workbook, import an XML file, and export data to an XML file. Finally, you'll work with data using Microsoft Query.

The files for this activity are in Student Data folder **Unit 5\Unit summary**.

1   Open East sales. (Verify that Export is the active worksheet.)

2   Export data from the Export worksheet to a text file. Save the text file as **My East sales**. (*Hint:* When prompted, export only the current sheet.)

3   Open the exported file in Notepad. (Because some product names are longer or shorter than others, the tabbed columns might not look neat.) Close Notepad.

4   Click the XML worksheet. Create a workbook map by using EmployeeRecord, and link the elements in the file to the corresponding fields in the workbook. (*Hint:* In the XML Source pane, click XML Maps.)

5   Import the EmployeeInfoPrac XML file.

6   Export the data in the XML worksheet as an XML file. Save the XML file as **My XML practice**.

7   Click the Exporting practice worksheet. Using Microsoft Query, select or create an Employee database connection. (*Hint:* On the Data tab, click From Other Sources and choose From Microsoft Query. If Employee does not appear in the Databases panel, select <New Data Source>; then click OK and enter data source information for the Employees database.)

8   Add all of the columns of the Employees table to your query.

9   Include only those records with a Dept code value that equals SL.

10 Sort the data by the last name (Lname) field, in ascending order.

11 Place the resulting data in cell A1 of the current sheet. Check the result against Exhibit 5-11.

12 Save the workbook as **My exporting practice** in Excel workbook format.

13 Close the XML Source pane.

14 Update and close the workbook.

⟋	A	B	C	D	E
1	Ecode ▾	Lname ▾	Fname ▾	Region ▾	Dept code ▾
2	E-02	Lee	Shannon	South	SL
3	E-03	McGregor	Melinda	West	SL
4	E-04	Overmire	James	North	SL
5	E-01	Pingault	Malcolm	East	SL

Exhibit 5-11: The worksheet as it appears after Step 11

Review questions

1 True or false? An Excel workbook that's saved in a different file format will retain its original formatting.

2 List three ways that the XML Source pane is useful.

3 How can you export a workbook to an XML file?

4 List the steps you would use to delete an XML map.

5 What is Microsoft Query?

6 What is the syntax for a cube function?

Unit 6

Analytical tools

Complete this unit, and you'll know how to:

A Use the Goal Seek and Solver utilities to meet a target output for a formula by changing the values in the input cells.

B Install and use the Analysis ToolPak.

C Create scenarios to save various sets of input values that produce different results.

Topic A: Goal Seek and Solver

This topic covers the following Microsoft Office Specialist objectives for exam 77-888: Excel Expert 2010.

#	Objective
3.2	**Apply data analysis**
	3.2.1 Use automated analysis tools
	3.2.2 Perform What-If analysis

What-if analysis

Explanation

You might want a formula to return a specific result, but you might not know the input values that will provide that result. For example, you might want to take out a loan for which the maximum monthly payment is $500. Based on this, you might want to know a possible combination of period, interest rate, and principal amount. In this case, you can use Goal Seek and Solver to find the input values.

You can use the Goal Seek and Solver utilities to perform a *what-if analysis*. This type of analysis involves changing the values in a worksheet and observing how these changes affect the results of the formulas. You use Goal Seek to solve problems that have one variable. Use Solver to analyze problems that have multiple variables and constraints.

The Goal Seek utility

Use the Goal Seek utility to solve a formula based on the value that you want the formula to return. To use the Goal Seek utility:

1   Click the Data tab.

2   In the Data Tools group, click What-If Analysis and choose Goal Seek to open the Goal Seek dialog box.

3   In the Set cell box, specify the cell that contains the formula you want to solve.

4   In the To value box, enter the result you want.

5   In the By changing cell box, specify the cell that contains the value you want to adjust.

6   Click OK.

Do it!

A-1: Using Goal Seek to solve for a single variable

The files for this activity are in Student Data folder **Unit 6\Topic A**.

Here's how	Here's why
1 Open Loan analysis	This workbook contains six worksheets. Goal seeking is the active sheet.
Save the workbook as **My loan analysis**	In the current topic folder.
2 Select E6	This cell displays a monthly payment of -$3,417.76 for a loan amount of $100,000. You'll use Goal Seek to calculate the loan amount that you can obtain if you can afford a monthly payment of $10,000, given a period of 36 months and an interest rate of 14%.
Observe the formula bar	f_x =PMT(D6%/12,C6,B6) The PMT function calculates the monthly payment for the loan amount in B6 based on the annual interest rate in D6 and the repayment period in C6.
3 Click the **Data** tab	
In the Data Tools group, click **What-If Analysis**	
Choose **Goal Seek...**	To open the Goal Seek dialog box. The Set cell box contains E6. This cell contains the formula you want to solve.
4 In the To value box, enter **-10000**	This is the result you want the formula in E6 to return.
In the "By changing cell" box, enter **B6**	This is the cell containing the loan amount: the value that will be adjusted.

5 Click **OK**

Goal Seek Status

Goal Seeking with Cell E6
found a solution.

Step

Target value: -10000
Current value: -$10,000.00

Pause

OK   Cancel

The Goal Seek Status dialog box opens. It states
that Goal Seek has found a solution, which you
can accept or reject. The target value is the value
you asked the formula to return. The current
value is the solution found by Goal Seek.

6 Click **OK**

To close the dialog box.

Institution	Loan amount (in $)	Period of repayment (in months)	Annual Rate of Interest (in %)	Monthly payment
Bank				
AmericaBank	$292,589	36	14	-$10,000.00

With a monthly payment of $10,000, a period of
36 months, and an interest rate of 14%, you can
afford a loan of $292,589.

7 Find the loan amount that you can
obtain from the NewCiti bank if
you pay $15,000 per month for 42
months

(Use Goal Seek.) You'll get $487,820 as the
loan amount.

8 Update the workbook

The Solver utility

Explanation

You use the Solver utility to perform complex what-if analyses. Solver helps you determine optimal values for a cell by adjusting multiple cells used in a formula. You can also apply multiple constraints to one or more cells used in a formula.

Although Solver is an add-in program, it is automatically installed with Excel 2010 and Office 2010. Before you can use the Solver add-in, though, you need to load it, or activate it.

To activate Solver and other add-ins:

1 On the Developer tab, click Add-Ins.

2 In the Add-Ins dialog box, shown in Exhibit 6-1, check Solver Add-In and any other add-ins you want to activate.

3 Click OK. The Solver button appears in the Analysis group on the Data tab. (If you don't see it, close and restart Excel.)

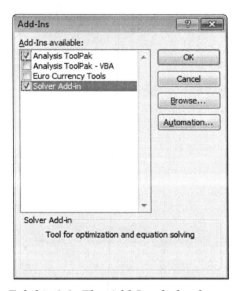

Exhibit 6-1: The Add-Ins dialog box

Do it!

A-2:   Activating Solver and the Analysis ToolPak

Here's how	Here's why
1 On the Developer tab, click **Add-Ins**	To open the Add-Ins dialog box. You'll activate the Solver and Analysis ToolPak add-ins.
2 Check **Analysis ToolPak** and **Solver Add-in**	As shown in Exhibit 6-1.
Click **OK**	To close the Add-Ins dialog box and activate the Analysis ToolPak and Solver Add-In.
3 Click the **Data** tab	To see that the Analysis group, with Data Analysis and Solver buttons, has been added.

Using Solver

Explanation

After you activate the Solver add-in, it's available on the Ribbon. To use the Solver utility:

1 On the Data tab, in the Analysis group, click Solver to open the Solver Parameters dialog box.

2 In the Set Objective box, specify the cell that contains the formula you want to solve.

3 Select the appropriate option—Max, Min, or Value Of—for the result of the target cell.

4 In the By Changing Variable Cells box, specify the cells in which the values will be adjusted.

5 In the Subject to the Constraints box, add any desired constraints by using the Add button. For example, if you were changing a cell that contained a period of months, you would want to constrain that cell to contain whole numbers. Exhibit 6-2 shows a solver model with three constraints.

6 From the Select a Solving Method list, select a method:

- GRG (Generalized Reduced Gradient) Nonlinear uses smooth nonlinear optimization.
- Simplex LP uses linear programming.
- Evolutionary uses non-smooth optimization.

7 Click Solve.

8 In the Solver Results dialog box, you can choose to Keep Solver Solutions or Restore Original Values.

9 Click OK.

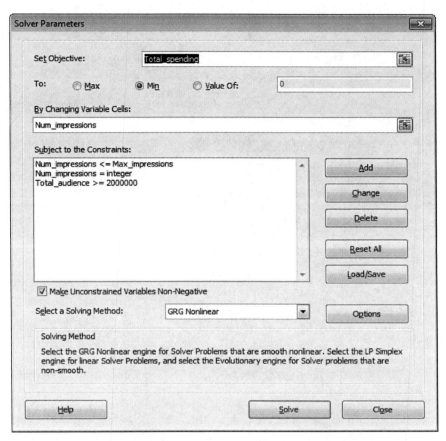

Exhibit 6-2: The Solver Parameters dialog box

Do it!

A-3: Using Solver to solve for multiple variables

Here's how	Here's why
1 In My loan analysis, click the Solver sheet	You'll use the Solver utility to minimize the company's advertising expenses while reaching an audience of 1 million people. You'll do this by adjusting the amounts spent on newspaper, radio, and TV ads.
2 Select each of the named ranges and observe the selected cells	This worksheet has ranges named Audience_reached, Max_impressions, Num_impressions, Spending, Total_audience, and Total_spending. Solver will show these names, rather than cell notations, to make the information easier to understand.
3 Click the **Data** tab	
In the Analysis group, click **Solver**	To open the Solver Parameters dialog box.
4 Select E15	(In the Solver sheet.) To enter it in the Set Objective box in the dialog box.
In the To area, select **Min**	To specify that you want to minimize the total spending.
5 Place the insertion point in the By Changing Variable Cells box	These are the cell values that Solver will adjust.
In the Solver sheet, select B14:D14	To make Solver change the values in this range in order to find the optimal advertising spending for each medium.
Press `TAB`	
6 Under Subject to the Constraints, click **Add**	To open the Add Constraint dialog box. You'll specify limitations for cell values based on your objectives.
7 Select E16	The total audience reached must be greater than or equal to 2 million.
From the comparison operator list, select **>=**	This is the greater-than-or-equal-to operator.
In the Constraint box, enter **2000000**	Cell Reference: $E$16 >= 2000000
Click **Add**	To add the constraint to the Subject to the Constraints list. The boxes in the Add Constraint dialog box are refreshed, and the insertion point is in the Cell Reference box.

8	Select B14:D14	The number of impressions for each cell in this range should be less than or equal to the maximum number of effective impressions listed above.
	In the list, verify that **<=** is selected	This is the less-than-or-equal-to operator.
	Click in the Constraint box	
	Select B10:D10	
		This range and the selected operator specify that the number of impressions must be less than the maximum effective number.
9	Click **Add**	
10	Select B14:D14	The number of impressions must be an integer; you can't purchase a fraction of an ad impression.
	From the operator list, select **int**	This is the integer operator.
	Click **OK**	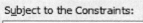
		To add this third constraint to the Subject to the Constraints list and return to the Solver Parameters dialog box. Total_spending appears in the Set Objective box, and Num_impressions appears in the By Changing Variable Cells box.
11	Click **Solve**	To make Solver find a set of values for the number of impressions needed to minimize the cost. The Solver Results dialog box appears.
	Observe the value in B14	The number of impressions for Newspaper is zero. You'll change a setting to prevent this problem.
	Select **Restore Original Values**	In the Solver Results dialog box.
	Check **Return to Solver Parameters Dialog**	
	Click **OK**	To return to the Solver Parameters dialog box, which shows the parameters you selected.

12 From the Select a Solving Method list, select **Simplex LP**

Select a Solving Method:	GRG Nonlinear
	GRG Nonlinear
Solving Method	Simplex LP
	Evolutionary

13 Click **Solve**

To tell Solver to adjust the values. After a moment, the Solver Results dialog box appears. Verify that Keep Solver Solution is selected; this ensures that the solution found by Solver is retained.

Clear **Return to Solver Parameters Dialog**

Click **OK**

The adjusted values appear in the worksheet. E15 shows the total spending as $17,700. The value in E16 is 2,000,000, and the number-of-impressions values are integers that are less than the corresponding maximum-effective-impressions values.

14 Update and close the workbook

Topic B: The Analysis ToolPak

This topic covers the following Microsoft Office Specialist objectives for exam 77-888: Excel Expert 2010.

#	Objective
3.2	**Apply data analysis**
	3.2.1 Use automated analysis tools

Available tools

Explanation

The Analysis ToolPak is a set of analysis tools, including Correlation, Covariance, Regression, and Sampling. Each tool consists of macro functions needed to perform the corresponding analysis. The following table lists the tools available in the ToolPak:

Analysis tool	Description
Anova	Performs variance analysis.
Correlation	Examines the relationship between two sets of data. Each set of data can have different units of measurement.
Covariance	Examines the relationship between two data ranges.
Descriptive Statistics	Summarizes information related to different types of data used in an analysis.
Exponential Smoothing	Adjusts the output based on previous forecasts.
F-Test Two Sample for Variances	Compares two population variances.
Fourier Analysis	Solves linear equations and analyzes periodic data by using the Fast Fourier Transform method.
Histogram	Determines the frequency of a value in a data range.
Moving Average	Forecasts values for a period based on the average of previous forecasts.
Random Number Generation	Generates random numbers based on several distributions to fill a range.
Rank and Percentile	Calculates the rank and percentile of each value in a data set.
Regression	Performs linear regression analysis to determine the relation between different values.
Sampling	Creates samples from a population.
t-Test	Tests the means of various populations.
z-Test	Tests the means of known variances.

Using analysis tools

After activating the Analysis ToolPak, you can select any tool from the Analysis Tools list. For example, you might want to create a sampling distribution for sales in a specific region for a specific year. To perform this analysis, you have to select samples from the sales report. You can use the Sampling analysis tool to get these samples from a data range. You can select data samples randomly or at regular intervals.

To select sample data by using the Sampling analysis tool:

1   Click the Data tab.
2   In the Analysis group, click Data Analysis to open the Data Analysis dialog box.
3   From the Analysis Tools list, select Sampling, and then click OK to open the Sampling dialog box.
4   In the Input Range box, enter the range of data from which you want to select samples.
5   Specify a sampling method and an output option.
6   Click OK.

Do it!

B-1: Using the Sampling analysis tool

The files for this activity are in Student Data folder **Unit 6\Topic B**.

Here's how	Here's why
1 Open Audit	
Save the workbook as **My audit**	
2 Observe the Sampling sheet	Outlander Spices needs to audit 15 quarterly sales values for several stores. You won't analyze that data in this activity, but you will randomly select the 15 store and quarter combinations by using the Sampling analysis tool.
	The Sampling sheet contains a list of stores and quarters, with a combination of both combined in a column (because the Sampling tool requires that the information be numeric). For example, 203 represents store 002's third-quarter sales.
3 Click the **Data** tab	If necessary.
In the Analysis group, click **Data Analysis**	To open the Data Analysis dialog box.
4 In the Analysis Tools list, select **Sampling**	You'll select data samples that represent sales in the East region.

Analysis Tools

F-Test Two-Sample for Variances
Fourier Analysis
Histogram
Moving Average
Random Number Generation
Rank and Percentile
Regression
Sampling
t-Test: Paired Two Sample for Means
t-Test: Two-Sample Assuming Equal Variances

5 Click **OK**	To open the Sampling dialog box.
6 In the Input Range box, enter **C7:C66**	(You can also click the Collapse Dialog button, select the range in the worksheet, and click the Expand Dialog button.) To specify the range of data from which samples are to be selected.
7 Under Sampling Method, select **Random**	(If necessary.) You'll select samples at random. Because the Sampling tool might repeat some values, you'll generate more than the target number of 15.
In the Number of Samples box, enter **20**	With 20 samples, 15 or more are likely to be unique.

8 Under Output options, select **Output Range**	You'll specify the range where the samples should appear. You can also display the output in a new worksheet or a new workbook.
In the Output Range box, enter **E7**	

```
Sampling
  Input
  Input Range:              $C$7:$C$66    [≣]
  ☐ Labels
  Sampling Method
  ○ Periodic
    Period:                 [          ]
  ● Random
    Number of Samples:      20
  Output options
  ● Output Range:           E7            [≣]
  ○ New Worksheet Ply:      [          ]
  ○ New Workbook
```

The output will begin in E7 and extend downward 20 rows.

9 Click **OK**	Data samples appear in E7:E26. Outlander Spices can now audit the quarterly sales values from the random sample you created.
10 Update and close the workbook	

Topic C: Scenarios

This topic covers the following Microsoft Office Specialist objectives for exam 77-882: Excel 2010.

#	Objective
1.3	**Personalize the environment by using Backstage**
	1.3.1 Manipulate the Quick Access Toolbar

This topic covers the following Microsoft Office Specialist objectives for exam 77-888: Excel Expert 2010.

#	Objective
3.2	**Apply data analysis**
	3.2.1 Use automated analysis tools
	3.2.2 Perform What-If analysis

Creating a scenario

Explanation

Scenarios are sets of input values that produce different results. For example, in a budget projection worksheet, you can have one scenario that includes conservative sales figures, and another scenario that includes more aggressive sales figures. Instead of creating new scenarios every time, you can modify existing scenarios. In a worksheet containing multiple scenarios, you can switch among them to view the results for different input values. In addition, you can merge scenarios from other worksheets.

You can use the Scenario Manager dialog box to create a scenario. Here's how:

1 Click the Data tab.
2 From the What-If Analysis menu in the Data Tools group, choose Scenario Manager to open the Scenario Manager dialog box.
3 Click the Add button to open the Add Scenario dialog box.
4 In the Scenario name box, enter a name for the scenario.
5 In the Changing cells box, specify the cells that contain the values you want to change. Click OK.
6 In the Scenario Values dialog box, specify values for the changing cells, and click OK.

After creating the scenario, you can modify it by editing values for the changing cells. To edit values:

1 Open the Scenario Manager dialog box and select the scenario you want to change.
2 Click Edit to open the Edit Scenario dialog box.
3 Click OK to open the Scenario Values dialog box.
4 Specify values for the changing cells and click OK.

Exhibit 6-3: The Scenario Manager dialog box

Do it!

C-1:   Creating scenarios

The files for this activity are in Student Data folder **Unit 6\Topic C**.

Here's how	Here's why
1 Open Projections	
Save the workbook as **My projections**	In the current topic folder.
2 Click the Scenarios sheet	(If necessary.) You'll create scenarios for this worksheet to see how different Cost-of-sales values will affect the Gross profit, Net profit, and Profit %.
3 Select B8:E8	The cost of sales for the four quarters.
Click the **Data** tab	If necessary.
From the What-If Analysis menu, choose **Scenario Manager…**	To open the Scenario Manager dialog box. Currently, no scenarios are defined.
Click **Add**	To open the Add Scenario dialog box.

4 In the Scenario name box, enter **Original profit**	This is the name of the scenario that will preserve the original values. The Changing cells box displays the references of the selected cells.
Edit the Comment box to read **Original projected profit**	To describe the scenario.
Click **OK**	

Scenario Values	
Enter values for each of the changing cells.	
1:	$B$8	25000
2:	$C$8	42050
3:	$D$8	59450
4:	$E$8	60450

To open the Scenario Values dialog box. All of the boxes display the current values of the selected cells.

5 Click **Add**	To add the Original profit scenario to the Scenarios list and return to the Add Scenario dialog box. This scenario will preserve the original values in changing cells.
6 In the Scenario name box, enter **Decreased cost of sales**	This is the name of the scenario you are about to create.
Edit the Comment box to read **Projected profit with decreased cost of sales**	To describe the new scenario.
Click **OK**	To open the Scenario Values dialog box.
7 Enter the values as shown	

Enter values for each of the changing cells.	
1:	$B$8	23000
2:	$C$8	40000
3:	$D$8	55000
4:	$E$8	55000

8 Click **OK**	To return to the Scenario Manager dialog box, shown in Exhibit 6-3. The Scenarios list displays the names of the two scenarios you just defined.
9 Click **Show**	To apply the "Decreased cost of sales" scenario. The values in the range B8:E8 change according to the values stored in this scenario. Based on the new Cost-of-sales values, the values for Gross profit, Net profit, and Profit % also change.
	You'll edit the scenario to lower the Cost-of-sales values even more.

10	Click **Edit**	To open the Edit Scenario dialog box. The Scenario name box contains "Decreased cost of sales."
	Click **OK**	To open the Scenario Values dialog box. All of the boxes display the current values of the selected cells.
11	Type the values shown	Enter values for each of the changing cells. 1: $B$8 20000 2: $C$8 35000 3: $D$8 50000 4: $E$8 48000
	Click **OK**	To return to the Scenario Manager dialog box.
	Click **Show**	To apply the changes made in the scenario.
	Click **Close**	The values for Cost of sales, Gross profit, Net profit, and Profit % have changed.
12	Update the workbook	

Switching among scenarios

Explanation You can switch among scenarios to view results based on different input values. To display a scenario, open the Scenario Manager dialog box, select the name of the scenario you want to display, and click the Show button.

If you have a worksheet with many scenarios, you can switch among them more easily by adding the Scenario list to the Quick Access toolbar. To add buttons to the Quick Access toolbar:

1 On the Quick Access toolbar, click Customize Quick Access Toolbar and choose More Commands. The Excel Options dialog box opens with the Quick Access Toolbar settings displayed.

2 From the Available commands list, select the category that contains the command you want to add, or select All Commands. Some commands are available only in the list of all commands.

3 Select the command you want to add to the toolbar and click Add.

4 If desired, click Move Up or Move Down to change the command's position relative to the other commands on the toolbar.

5 Click OK to close the Excel Options dialog box.

Do it! ## C-2: Switching among scenarios

Here's how	Here's why
1 Observe F15	The Profit % is 36.
2 On the Quick Access toolbar, click as shown	To display the Customize Quick Access Toolbar menu.
Choose **More Commands...**	To open the Excel Options dialog box, with the Quick Access Toolbar page active.
3 From the "Choose commands from" list, select **Data tab**	The Scenario Manager is on the Data tab.
4 In the list of commands, select **Scenario Manager...**	The commands are listed in alphabetical order.
In the Customize Quick Access Toolbar list, verify that **For all documents (default)** is selected	To ensure that the button you'll add is available in all documents, not just the active one.

5 Click **Add**	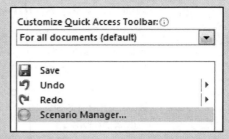 To add the command to the Quick Access toolbar.
6 From the "Choose commands from" list, select **All commands**	
7 In the list of commands, select **Scenario**	
Click **Add**	To add the command to the Quick Access toolbar.
8 Click **OK**	To close the Excel Options dialog box.
9 On the Quick Access toolbar, click as shown	 To open the Scenario Manager dialog box.
Select **Original profit**	
Click **Show**	To display the Original profit scenario. In cell F15, the Profit % is 25.
Click **Close**	
10 On the Quick Access toolbar, click as shown	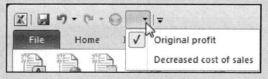 To display the Scenario list.
Select **Decreased cost of sales**	You can use this list to switch among scenarios.
11 Update the workbook	

Merging scenarios

Explanation

You can merge scenarios from different worksheets so that all scenarios in a source worksheet are copied to the active worksheet. The changing cells in the active worksheet correspond to those in the source worksheet. This ensures that the changes made in the source worksheet are reflected in the active worksheet.

To merge scenarios:

1 Click the worksheet where you want to merge scenarios.
2 Open the Scenario Manager dialog box.
3 Click Merge.
4 From the Sheet list, select the worksheet that contains the scenarios you want to merge.
5 Click OK.

The Scenario Summary report

A Scenario Summary report displays the original and current values for the changing cells corresponding to available scenarios. To create a Scenario Summary report:

1 Open the Scenario Manager dialog box.
2 Click Summary to open the Scenario Summary dialog box.
3 In the Result cells box, select the cells that contain the values changed by scenarios.
4 Click OK.

Scenario Summary		Current Values:	Original profit	Decreased cost of sales
Changing Cells:				
$B$8		20000	25000	20000
$C$8		35000	42050	35000
$D$8		50000	59450	50000
$E$8		48000	60450	48000
Result Cells:				
$E$8		48000	60450	48000
$C$9		43200	36150	43200
Notes: Current Values column represents values of changing cells at time Scenario Summary Report was created. Changing cells for each scenario are highlighted in gray.				

Exhibit 6-4: A sample Scenario Summary

Do it!

C-3: Merging scenarios from another worksheet

Here's how	Here's why
1 Click the Scenarios 2 sheet	You'll merge scenarios to this worksheet from the Scenarios worksheet.
Observe F15	The Profit % is 25.
2 Open the Scenario Manager dialog box	(Click the Scenario Manager button on the Quick Access toolbar.) There are no scenarios in the Scenarios 2 worksheet.

3 Click **Merge**	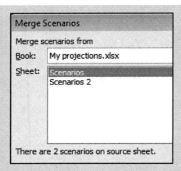
	To open the Merge Scenarios dialog box. The Book box displays the name of the workbook from which you'll merge scenarios. The Sheet list contains the worksheets in the workbook.
Verify that **Scenarios** is selected	You'll merge the scenarios in this worksheet.
4 Click **OK**	To return to the Scenario Manager dialog box. The Scenarios list displays the names of the two scenarios you just merged. By default, Original profit is selected.
5 Select **Decreased cost of sales** and click **Show**	To apply the "Decreased cost of sales" scenario. The values for Cost of sales, Gross profit, Net profit, and Profit % change according to the values stored in the scenario.
Observe F15	The Profit % has increased to 36% in the Scenarios 2 worksheet.
6 Click **Summary**	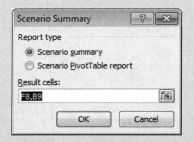
	To open the Scenario Summary dialog box. By default, Scenario summary is selected.
In the worksheet, select E8	
Hold (CTRL) and select C9	To add it to the Result cells list. The values in these cells changed when you applied the "Decreased cost of sales" scenario.
Click **OK**	To create the Scenario Summary report in a new worksheet. You'll see the original and current values in the changing cells and result cells.
7 Update and close the workbook	

Unit summary: Analytical tools

Topic A   In this topic, you used **Goal Seek** to find a specific result for a formula by changing the value of one of the input cells. You also used the **Solver** add-in to determine optimal values for a cell by changing the values of multiple cells used in a formula.

Topic B   In this topic, you installed and used the **Analysis ToolPak**. You also used the Sampling analysis tool to select samples from a data range.

Topic C   In this topic, you created and edited **scenarios**. You learned that scenarios are used to save sets of input values that produce different results. Then, you switched among scenarios to view different data results in a worksheet. In addition, you merged scenarios and created a Scenario Summary report.

Independent practice activity

In this activity, you'll use Goal Seek and Solver to calculate values. You'll also create and display several views.

The files for this activity are in Student Data folder **Unit 6\Unit summary**.

1 Open Employee loan. Goal seeking should be the active worksheet.

2 Save the workbook as **My employee loan**.

3 In D6, use Goal Seek to calculate the loan amount in C6 for a monthly deduction of **$2,300**. (*Hint:* Cell C6 is the cell to be changed. The loan amount will be $108,250.)

4 Click the Solver worksheet. Use Solver to calculate a total profit of **30%** by adjusting the values for Total sales, Cost of sales, Overhead, and Marketing. When adjusting values, you must ensure that the total overhead for the year cannot be **greater than $25,000**, and the net profit for the year must be **at least $100,000**. Compare your results with Exhibit 6-5. (*Hint:* The Solver Parameters dialog box should look like the one shown in Exhibit 6-6.)

5 Update and close the workbook.

	A	B	C	D	E	F
1	**Outlander Spices**					
2	**Profit projection**					
3						
4						
5		Qtr1	Qtr2	Qtr3	Qtr4	Total
6						
7	Total sales	$51,408	$81,644	$94,011	$107,592	$334,655
8	Cost of sales	$25,115	$42,376	$60,102	$61,124	$188,717
9	Gross profit	$26,293	$39,268	$33,909	$46,468	$145,938
10						
11	Overhead	$7,510	$7,530	$5,626	$3,522	$24,189
12	Marketing	$7,009	$6,638	$4,504	$3,202	$21,353
13		$14,519	$14,169	$10,130	$6,724	$45,542
14	Net profit	$11,773	$25,099	$23,780	$39,744	$100,396
15	Profit %	23	31	25	37	30

Exhibit 6-5: The Solver worksheet after Step 4

Exhibit 6-6: The Solver Parameters dialog box after Step 4

Review questions

1 What utilities can be used to perform what-if analyses?

2 Which utility solves a formula based on the value that you want the formula to return?

3 List the steps you would use to install the Analysis ToolPak.

4 What are scenarios?

5 List the steps you would use to change a scenario.

Unit 7

Macros and custom functions

Complete this unit, and you'll know how to:

A Create and run macros to automate complex and repetitive tasks.

B Use the Visual Basic Editor to edit a macro.

C Create custom functions.

Topic A: Running and recording a macro

This topic covers the following Microsoft Office Specialist objectives for exam 77-882: Excel 2010.

#	Objective
1.3	**Personalize the environment by using Backstage**
	1.3.1 Manipulate the Quick Access Toolbar
	1.3.2 Customize the Ribbon
	1.3.2.2 Groups

This topic covers the following Microsoft Office Specialist objectives for exam 77-888: Excel Expert 2010.

#	Objective
4.1	**Create and manipulate macros**
	4.1.1 Run a macro
	4.1.2 Run a macro when a workbook is opened
	4.1.3 Run a macro when a button is clicked
	4.1.4 Record an action macro
	4.1.5 Assign a macro to a command button
	4.1.6 Create a custom macro button on the Quick Access Toolbar
4.2	**Insert and manipulate form controls**
	4.2.1 Insert form controls
	4.2.2 Set form properties

Running macros

Explanation

You can use macros to automate complex and repetitive tasks. A *macro* is a series of instructions that execute automatically with a single command. For example, you can create a macro to format a worksheet or to print a report. You can use the macros already available in Excel or create your own. To make macros more convenient to use, you can assign them to Quick Access toolbar buttons.

To run a macro, click the Developer tab. In the Code group, click Macros to open the Macro dialog box, shown in Exhibit 7-1. Select the desired macro and click Run.

Exhibit 7-1: The Macro dialog box

Enabling macros

Macros can contain viruses that can harm your computer. To combat this problem, Excel requires you to enable macros after opening a file that contains them. To enable macros, click Enable Content in the Security Warning bar that appears.

If Windows is set to display file-name extensions, you can use them to distinguish an Excel file that contains macros from an Excel file without macros. A standard Excel 2010 file uses the extension .xlsx; an Excel 2010 file with macro code uses the extension .xlsm.

Trust Center macro settings

You can protect your computer from potentially dangerous macros by using one of the following macro settings in the Trust Center:

- Disable all macros without notification
- Disable all macros with notification (default setting)
- Disable all macros except digitally signed macros
- Enable all macros (not recommended)

To change the default setting, click Macro Security in the Code group on the Developer tab. The Trust Center dialog box opens, with Macro Settings selected in the left pane. Select the desired macro security setting and click OK.

Do it!

A-1: Running a macro

The files for this activity are in Student Data folder **Unit 7\Topic A**.

Here's how	Here's why
1 Open Running macros	This document contains macros, which are disabled by default. You'll enable the macros so you can run them.
In the Security Warning bar that appears, click **Enable Content**	(Above the formula bar.) To enable the macros included in the workbook.

> ⚠ **Security Warning**   Macros have been disabled.   **Enable Content**

2 Open the Save As dialog box	
In the File name box, enter **My macros**	
Observe that Excel Macro-Enabled Workbook is selected in the Save as type list	File <u>n</u>ame: My macros Save as <u>t</u>ype: Excel Macro-Enabled Workbook
	Excel 2010 files with macros are saved as a different file type, with the extension .xlsm instead of .xlsx.
Click **Save**	To save the file in the current topic folder.
3 Select A4:D4	You'll run the Column_titles macro to wrap the text in the selected cells.
On the Developer tab, in the Code group, click **Macros**	To open the Macro dialog box. It lists the names of available macros, as shown in Exhibit 7-1.
Observe that the Column_titles macro is selected	
Click **Run**	To run the macro. Notice that the text in the cells is wrapped to multiple lines as necessary, bottom-aligned, and bold.
4 Select E4	The macros in this workbook were assigned shortcut keys. You'll use one to run the Column_titles macro.
Press (CTRL) + (SHIFT) + (C)	The text is formatted to match the other column titles.
5 Select E5	The cell for Michael Lee's monthly deduction amount.
Run the Monthly_deduction macro	(Use the Macro dialog box.) The monthly deduction amount appears in E5.

6 Select E5	f_x =PMT(10%/12,D5,-C5)
	The formula for the PMT function appears in the formula bar. This formula was entered by the macro you just ran.
7 Display the monthly deduction for James Overmire in E6	Use the shortcut key Ctrl+Shift+M to run the Monthly_deduction macro.
8 Update and close the workbook	

Recording macros

Explanation

To create a macro, you can write the Visual Basic code for it, or you can have Excel record actions as you perform them. Recording is simpler, but creates more lines of code; this can be less efficient if you want to edit the macro later.

To record a macro:

1 In the status bar, click the Record Macro button to open the Record Macro dialog box.

2 Specify a macro name and a shortcut key. Macro names can include letters, numbers, and underscores. Names must begin with a letter and cannot contain spaces.

3 Click OK to start recording the macro.

4 Perform the actions you want to include in the macro. As you work, Excel records the sequence of steps.

5 When you're finished, click the Stop Recording button in the status bar.

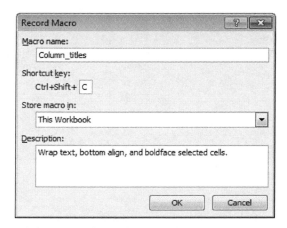

Exhibit 7-2: The Column_titles macro in the Record Macro dialog box

Saving files with macros

When you add a macro to a file that didn't contain any and you then save the file, Excel displays a message box, warning you that it will save the file without macros. The default Yes response will delete any macros you've recorded. Click No to stop saving; then choose File, Save As and save the file in the Excel Macro-Enabled Workbook format.

Do it!

A-2:   Recording a macro

The files for this activity are in Student Data folder **Unit 7\Topic A**.

Here's how	Here's why
1 Open Loan details	You'll record a macro to format column titles.
2 Save the workbook as **My loan details**	
3 Select E4	This cell should be formatted as a column heading. When you want a macro to be associated with a particular cell, select that cell before turning on the recorder.
In the status bar, click	To open the Record Macro dialog box.
4 Edit the Macro name box to read **Column_titles**	
Click in the Shortcut key box	
Press (SHIFT) + (C)	Shortcut key: Ctrl+Shift+ c
	To define the shortcut key for the Column_titles macro as Ctrl+Shift+C. (Excel adds the Ctrl part.)
In the "Store macro in" list, verify that **This Workbook** is selected	To specify that the macro will be stored in only the active workbook.
In the Description box, enter **Wrap text, bottom align, and boldface selected cells.**	As shown in Exhibit 7-2.
5 Click **OK**	The Stop Recording button appears in the status bar.
6 Click the **Home** tab	If necessary.
In the Alignment group, click Wrap Text	To make the text wrap to multiple lines.
Click	To left-align the text in the cell.
Click	To position the text at the bottom of the cell.
In the Font group, click **B**	To apply bold formatting. You've completed all of the steps you want the macro to perform.

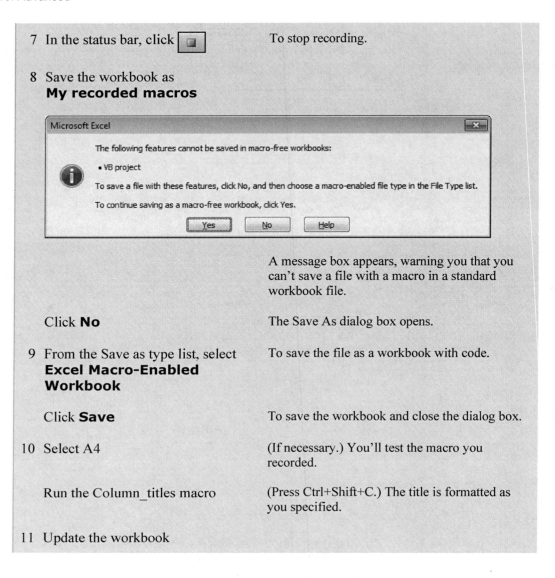

7 In the status bar, click ▣   To stop recording.

8 Save the workbook as
My recorded macros

> Microsoft Excel
>
> ⓘ The following features cannot be saved in macro-free workbooks:
>
> • VB project
>
> To save a file with these features, click No, and then choose a macro-enabled file type in the File Type list.
>
> To continue saving as a macro-free workbook, click Yes.
>
>   Yes   No   Help

     A message box appears, warning you that you can't save a file with a macro in a standard workbook file.

Click **No**   The Save As dialog box opens.

9 From the Save as type list, select   To save the file as a workbook with code.
Excel Macro-Enabled Workbook

Click **Save**   To save the workbook and close the dialog box.

10 Select A4   (If necessary.) You'll test the macro you recorded.

Run the Column_titles macro   (Press Ctrl+Shift+C.) The title is formatted as you specified.

11 Update the workbook

Assigning macros to command buttons

Explanation

There are several ways to run a macro. One of them is to assign a macro to a button on the Quick Access toolbar; you can then run the macro by clicking that button.

Adding a macro button to the Quick Access Toolbar

To assign a macro to a button:

1   Click the Customize Quick Access Toolbar button and choose More Commands. The Excel Options dialog box opens with the Quick Access Toolbar settings displayed.

2   From the "Choose commands from" list, select Macros.

3   Select the macro you want to add to the toolbar and click Add.

4   Click OK.

Adding a macro button to the Ribbon

To create a new Ribbon group for your custom macros:

1   Right-click the Ribbon and choose Customize the Ribbon. (You can also click the File tab, choose Options, and then select Customize the Ribbon.)

2   From the "Choose commands from" list, select Macros.

3   Under Main Tabs, select the Developer tab, and then click New Group.

4   Select the item named New Group (Custom) and click Rename.

5   Enter a new name for the group, such as My Macros, and click OK.

6   From the macro list, select the macro you want to add to the Ribbon.

7   Click Add. The macro appears under the new group.

8   Click OK. The macro button appears in the new group on the Developer tab.

Do it!   ## A-3:   Assigning a macro to a command button

Here's how	Here's why
1 On the Quick Access toolbar, click as shown	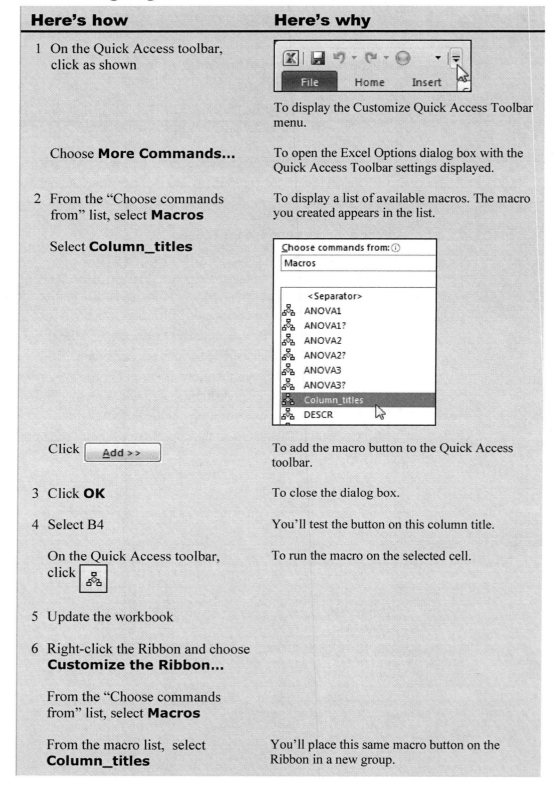
	To display the Customize Quick Access Toolbar menu.
Choose **More Commands...**	To open the Excel Options dialog box with the Quick Access Toolbar settings displayed.
2 From the "Choose commands from" list, select **Macros**	To display a list of available macros. The macro you created appears in the list.
Select **Column_titles**	
Click **Add >>**	To add the macro button to the Quick Access toolbar.
3 Click **OK**	To close the dialog box.
4 Select B4	You'll test the button on this column title.
On the Quick Access toolbar, click	To run the macro on the selected cell.
5 Update the workbook	
6 Right-click the Ribbon and choose **Customize the Ribbon...**	
From the "Choose commands from" list, select **Macros**	
From the macro list, select **Column_titles**	You'll place this same macro button on the Ribbon in a new group.

7 In the Main Tabs list, verify that the **Developer** tab is selected

Main Tabs
- ☑ Home
  - ⊞ Clipboard
  - ⊞ Font
  - ⊞ Alignment
  - ⊞ Number
  - ⊞ Styles
  - ⊞ Cells
  - ⊞ Editing
- ⊞ ☑ Insert
- ⊞ ☑ Page Layout
- ⊞ ☑ Formulas
- ⊞ ☑ Data
- ⊞ ☑ Review
- ⊞ ☑ View
- ⊞ ☑ Developer
- ⊞ ☑ Add-Ins
- ⊞ ☑ Background Removal

Click **New Group**

(The New Group button is below the Main Tabs list.) A new group is added to the Developer tab.

8 Select **New Group (Custom)**

You'll rename this group.

Click **Rename**

In the Display Name box, enter **My Macros**

Display name: My Macros

Click **OK**

9 Verify that the **Column_titles** macros is selected

Click Add >>

- ☑ Developer
  - ⊞ Code
  - ⊞ Add-Ins
  - ⊞ Controls
  - ⊞ XML
  - ⊞ Modify
  - My Macros (Custom)
    - Column_titles
- ⊞ ☑ Add-Ins

To add the macro button to the new My Macros group on the Developer tab.

10 Click **OK**

To close the Excel Options dialog box. You'll test the button on another column title.

11 Select C4

In the My Macros group, click the
Column_titles button

To run the macro on the selected cell.

12 Update the workbook

Inserting macro buttons in the worksheet

Explanation

To run a macro by clicking a button in the worksheet, you need to assign a macro to the specific button or shape object. You can either insert a new button and assign a macro to it, or assign a macro to an existing object.

To assign a macro to an existing object, right-click the object and choose Assign Macro. Then select the macro and click OK.

To insert a button (a form control) and assign a macro to it, use the following steps:

1 On the Developer tab, in the Controls group, click Insert.
2 From the Form Controls list, select Button (Form Control).
3 Drag to draw the button in the worksheet. When you release the mouse, the Assign Macro dialog box appears.
4 Select the macro you want to run when the button is clicked.
5 Click OK.

Exhibit 7-3: Inserting a form control

Modifying the button (form control) properties

Once the button has been inserted, you can edit the button text and change its appearance, as with any other Excel object. To select the button without running the assigned macro, right-click the button.

From the shortcut menu, you can do the following:

- Choose Edit Text to change the button text.
- Choose Assign Macro to change the assigned macro.
- Choose Format Control to open the Format Control dialog box, shown in Exhibit 7-4. Use the Font, Alignment, Size, Protection, Properties, Margins, and Alt Text tabs to format the button.

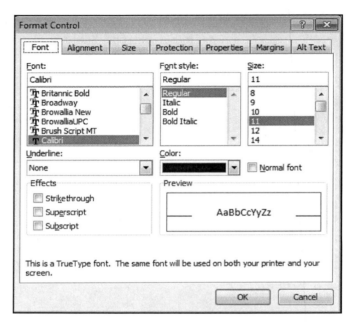

Exhibit 7-4: The Format Control dialog box

Do it!

A-4: Inserting a macro button

Here's how	Here's why
1 On the Developer tab, in the Controls group, click **Insert**	Insert To display a gallery of controls.
2 Click **Button (Form Control)**, as shown	Form Controls Button (Form Control) The mouse pointer changes to a crosshair.

3 In an empty area of the worksheet, drag to draw a button	The exact size is not important.
Release the mouse pointer	The Assign Macro dialog box appears.
4 From the Macro Name list, select **Column_titles**	To assign this macro to the newly drawn button.
Click **OK**	To close the Assign Macro dialog box. "Button 1" appears on the new button.
5 Right-click the button and choose **Edit Text**	You'll change the button text to be more descriptive.
Enter **Format Column Titles**	

> Format Column Titles

If the button is too small, drag the lower-right corner handle to increase the size of the button and display the button text.

Click the worksheet	To deselect the button.
6 Right-click the button and choose **Format Control**	You can use the settings on these seven tabs to control the appearance of the button.
Click **Cancel**	
7 Select D4	
Click the **Format Column Titles** button	To format the column title "No. of monthly payments" in D4.
8 Update the workbook	

Creating an Auto_Open macro

Explanation

You can create a macro that runs when a workbook is opened. You must name the macro Auto_Open to force it to run when the workbook is opened. There can be only one Auto_Open macro in a workbook.

To create an Auto_Open macro:

1 On the Developer tab, in the Code group, click Record Macro.
2 In the Name box, enter Auto_Open.
3 From the Store macro in list, select the desired location:
   - **Personal Macro Workbook** — Is a hidden workbook (Personal.xlsb) that is stored in the User/*User name*/AppData/Roaming/Microsoft/Excel/XLStart folder. The macro will run whenever Excel starts.
   - **This Workbook** — Stores the macro in the current workbook and runs when the workbook is opened.
   - **New Workbook** — Runs the Auto_Open macro whenever a new workbook is created.
4 Enter a description, if desired.
5 Click OK.
6 Perform the steps that you want the macro to record.
7 Click Stop Recording.
8 Save and close the workbook.

Enabling macros

While working on macros, you will need to enable all macros in the workbook. Because enabling macros can be harmful to your system, Microsoft recommends that you return to the default macro settings when you are finished creating and testing your macros.

To enable all macros:

1 On the Developer tab, in the Code group, click Macro Security.
2 Select Macro Settings (if necessary).
3 Select "Enable all macros (not recommended; potentially dangerous code can run)."
4 Click OK.

Do it!

A-5: Creating an Auto_Open macro

Here's how	Here's why
1 In the status bar, click [icon]	To start recording an Auto_Open macro that clears all the formatting from the worksheet when it's opened.
2 In the Macro name box, enter **Auto_Open**	

3 In the Description box, enter
   Clears all formats

Macro name:

Auto_Open

Shortcut key:

Ctrl+

Store macro in:

This Workbook

Description:

Clears all formats

   Click **OK**

4 Select the entire worksheet

	A
1	

5 On the Home tab, in the Editing
   group, click **Clear** and choose
   Clear Formats

6 Select A1   To deselect the entire worksheet

7 Click 🔲

8 Save the workbook as
   My open macro

9 Use the macro button to format
   the column titles

   Update and close the workbook

10 Open My open macro   The column file formatting is still applied. Since
                                         this is the first time you have opened this file,
                                         Excel will not run macros without confirmation.

    In the Security Warning bar, click   The Auto_Open macro runs and clears the
    Enable Content   column title formatting.

    Update and close the workbook

Topic B: Working with VBA code

This topic covers the following Microsoft Office Specialist objectives for exam 77-888: Excel Expert 2010.

#	Objective
4.1	**Create and manipulate macros**
	4.1.7 Apply modifications to a macro

Examining VBA code

Explanation

Excel saves the steps in a macro as Visual Basic for Applications (VBA) code. You can view and edit the code for a macro with the Visual Basic Editor.

VBA code is stored in special sheets called *modules*. A module might contain one or more sub procedures. A *sub procedure* is a named block of lines of code which, when executed, perform a sequence of steps.

VBA code consists of statements and comments. *Statements* are instructions that perform certain actions. *Comments* are non-executable lines of text used to describe sections of macro code. Comments begin with an apostrophe.

The following table describes the components of a statement:

Item	Description
Keywords	Special VBA terms that, by default, appear in blue. For example, the Sub keyword marks the beginning of a sub procedure, and the End Sub keyword marks the end of a sub procedure.
Variables	Used to store values. For example, you can use variables to store the results of a formula.
Operators	Used just as they are in a worksheet. Operators can be arithmetic (+, -, /, *) or comparison (=, >, <).
Procedure call	A statement that calls a procedure from another procedure. You can do this by inserting the name of the procedure you're calling into the procedure you are calling it from.

Observing a VBA code module

To observe a VBA code module, open the Macro dialog box. Then click the Edit button to open the Microsoft Visual Basic window. To close the code window, choose File, Close and Return to Microsoft Excel.

Do it!   **B-1:   Observing a VBA code module**

The files for this activity are in Student Data folder **Unit 7\Topic B**.

Here's how	Here's why
1 Open Outlander Spices	
Click **Enable Content**	To enable the macros contained in this workbook.
Save the macro-enabled workbook as **My Outlander Spices**	In the current topic folder.
2 Open the Macro dialog box	(On the Developer tab, in the Code group, click Macros.) By default, Column_titles is selected in the Macro name list.
Click **Edit**	To open the Microsoft Visual Basic window. The workbook's name appears in the title bar.
Observe the Code window	This window displays the code for the Column_titles macro.
3 Observe the first line in the Code window	``` Sub Column_titles() ``` The Sub keyword marks the beginning of the macro. Keywords are shown in blue.
Observe the last line in the Code window	``` End Sub ``` The End Sub keyword marks the end of the macro.
4 Observe the comments	``` ' Column_titles Macro ' Wrap text, bottom align, and boldface sel| ' ' Keyboard Shortcut: Ctrl+Shift+C ``` Comments begin with an apostrophe and describe the macro. By default, comments are green.
5 Observe the statements	Statements appear in black and instruct Excel to perform a sequence of actions. The statements are located between the Sub and End Sub keywords.
Observe the indented statement lines between the first set of With Selection and End With lines	Each group of lines between the With Selection and End With statements applies to the selected cells. Sophisticated macros can select cells other than the ones originally selected when the macro was created.
Observe the repeats of the With Selection/End With blocks	Each time you clicked a button in the Alignment group, the macro recorded all of the alignment settings. This isn't an efficient use of code because many of the lines are repeated.

Editing VBA code

Explanation

Sometimes you might need to edit the code for a macro. For example, say you have a macro that calculates the monthly deduction at an interest rate of 12%, and you want to change the interest rate to 11%. Instead of recording a new macro, you can edit the VBA code of the existing macro.

You can edit macro code in the Visual Basic Editor. Make sure you save the macro after you've made any necessary changes.

Do it!

B-2: Editing VBA code

Here's how	Here's why
1 In the three `With Selection` blocks of code, compare the `.WrapText`, `.HorizontalAlignment`, and `.VerticalAlignment` lines	Excel created each block of code when you clicked a button in the Alignment group. The first block set the `.WrapText` value to `True`, the second block set the `.HorizontalAlignment` value to `xlLeft`, and the third block set the `.VerticalAlignment` setting to `xlBottom`.
	Because the third block contains the settings you chose for the first two, the first two are redundant. You'll delete them to make the code more efficient.
2 Select from the first instance of `With Selection` through the second instance of `End With`, as shown	
	These blocks of code are no longer necessary.
3 Press ⟨DELETE⟩	To delete the selected code.
	You've decided that you don't want the macro to change the horizontal alignment, so you'll delete that code as well.

```
' Keyboard Shortcut: Ctrl+Shift+C
'
    With Selection
        .HorizontalAlignment = xlRight
        .VerticalAlignment = xlTop
        .WrapText = True
        .Orientation = 0
        .AddIndent = False
        .IndentLevel = 0
        .ShrinkToFit = False
        .ReadingOrder = xlContext
        .MergeCells = False
    End With
    With Selection
        .HorizontalAlignment = xlLeft
        .VerticalAlignment = xlTop
        .WrapText = True
        .Orientation = 0
        .AddIndent = False
        .IndentLevel = 0
        .ShrinkToFit = False
        .ReadingOrder = xlContext
        .MergeCells = False
    End With
    With Selection
        .HorizontalAlignment = xlLeft
        .VerticalAlignment = xlBottom
        .WrapText = True
```

4 Delete the following line:

```
.HorizontalAlignment = xlLeft
```

Compare your code with the code
shown below

```
Sub Column_titles()
'
' Column_titles Macro
' Wrap text, bottom align, and boldface selected cells.
'
' Keyboard Shortcut: Ctrl+Shift+C
'

    With Selection
        |
        .VerticalAlignment = xlBottom
        .WrapText = True
        .Orientation = 0
        .AddIndent = False
        .IndentLevel = 0
        .ShrinkToFit = False
        .ReadingOrder = xlContext
        .MergeCells = False
    End With
    Selection.Font.Bold = True
End Sub
```

5 Click 💾   To update the code.

Choose **File**, **Close and**   To close the Microsoft Visual Basic window.
Return to Microsoft Excel

6 Update and close the workbook

Topic C: Creating functions

Explanation

A *function procedure* is similar to a sub procedure except that the function procedure returns a value on execution. All of the built-in functions in Excel, such as SUM and AVERAGE, are written with function procedures.

You can also create functions to meet your specific needs. Such functions are called *custom functions*. For example, you can create a function that calculates commissions for salespeople based on their total sales.

Custom functions

You create custom functions in a Visual Basic module. In a custom function, you can include mathematical expressions, built-in Excel functions, and Visual Basic code. You can create custom functions to work with text, numbers, or dates.

You use custom functions in the same way you use built-in functions. You can also supply values to a custom function. That function then performs calculations on those values and returns a result.

Parts of a custom function

Examine the following code:

```
Function Profit(sales, cost)
Profit=sales-cost
End Function
```

Here, the Function keyword marks the beginning of the function. Profit is the name of the function, and the End Function keyword marks the end of the function.

Arguments are the values that a function uses for calculations. Arguments are specified in parentheses after the function name. In the preceding code, sales and cost are the arguments of the Profit function.

A *return value* is the value returned by a function after execution. You specify the return value by equating the function name to the value it must return. This is shown in the second statement of the preceding code (Profit=sales-cost).

Creating modules

A workbook can contain more than one Visual Basic module. Adding modules can help you organize code if you've created many macros or custom functions. To create an additional module, open the Microsoft Visual Basic window and choose Insert, Module.

Do it!

C-1: Creating a custom function

The files for this activity are in Student Data folder **Unit 7\Topic C**.

Here's how	Here's why
1 Open Loan deductions	
Click **Enable Content**	To enable the macros contained in this workbook.
Save the macro-enabled workbook as **My loan deductions**	In the current topic folder.

2 Click the **Developer** tab   If necessary.

3 In the Code group, click   To open the Microsoft Visual Basic window.
   Visual Basic

4 Choose **Insert, Module**   To add a module sheet.

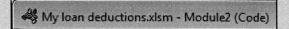
My loan deductions.xlsm - Module2 (Code)

In the title bar, Module2 indicates that this is the second module in the My loan deductions workbook.

5 Place the insertion point in the   If necessary.
   Code window

6 Enter the following code:

```
Function MyDeduction(loan_amt, num_pmts)
```

This code defines a function named MyDeduction in which loan_amt and num_pmts are the arguments.

   Press (↵ ENTER)   To move to the next row. The keyword End Function appears automatically at the end.

7 Enter the following code:

```
MyDeduction = -pmt(0.1/12, num_pmts, loan_amt)
```

This code calculates the payment based on 10% annual interest (expressed as 0.1 divided by 12 months), and returns the result.

8 Update the code   Click the Save button.

   Close the Microsoft Visual Basic   Choose File, Close and Return to Microsoft
   window   Excel.

9 In E5, enter   The payment of $1,816.62 appears in E5.
   =MyDeduction(C5,D5)

10 Update and close the workbook

Unit summary: Macros and custom functions

Topic A   In this topic, you recorded and ran a **macro**. You learned that macros perform tasks automatically and can be created to meet your specific needs. Then you assigned a macro to a **command button** as well as to a button inserted into the worksheet. You also added a macro button to the Quick Access toolbar and to the Ribbon. You created an **Auto_Open** macro that runs when the workbook is opened.

Topic B   In this topic, you learned that macros are saved as **VBA code**, and you examined some VBA code. Then you edited the code for a macro.

Topic C   In this topic, you created a **custom function**. You learned that custom functions are used to perform calculations when built-in functions are not available for your purposes.

Independent practice activity

In this activity, you'll record, edit, and run several macros.

The files for this activity are in Student Data folder **Unit 7\Unit summary**.

1 Open Outlander profit. (*Hint:* The Macros worksheet contains two scenarios: Original and Lower cost of sales. To access these scenarios, you'll click the Data tab.)

2 Save the workbook as **My Outlander profit** in the Excel Macro-Enabled Workbook file format.

3 Record a macro named **Display_lower_cost_of_sales** that has Ctrl+Shift+C as its shortcut key. This macro should show the "Lower cost of sales" scenario.

   To do this, start recording the macro. Click the Data tab, click What-If Analysis, and choose Scenario Manager. In the Scenarios list, select **Lower cost of sales**, and then click **Show**. Click **Close**; then stop recording the macro.

4 Record a macro named **Display_original** that has Ctrl+Shift+O as its shortcut key. This macro should show the Original scenario.

5 Run the Display_lower_cost_of_sales macro. Run the Display_original macro.

6 Change the name of the "Lower cost of sales" scenario to **Decreased cost of sales**. (*Hint:* Open the Scenario Manager dialog box, select **Lower cost of sales** from the Scenarios list, and click **Edit**. Do not change any other values.)

7 Edit the VBA code for the Display_lower_cost_of_sales macro to show the "Decreased cost of sales" scenario. (*Hint:* Edit the macro by replacing the argument of the ActiveSheet.Scenarios function with **Decreased cost of sales**.) Compare your VBA code window to Exhibit 7-5.

8 Update the VBA code and close the Microsoft Visual Basic window.

9 Run the edited macro.

10 Update the workbook and close it.

11 Close Excel.

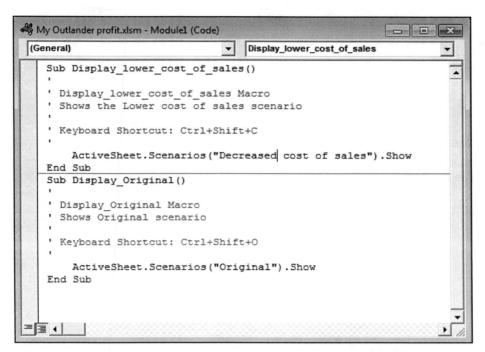

Sub Display_lower_cost_of_sales()

```
Sub Display_lower_cost_of_sales()
'
' Display_lower_cost_of_sales Macro
' Shows the Lower cost of sales scenario
'
' Keyboard Shortcut: Ctrl+Shift+C
'
    ActiveSheet.Scenarios("Decreased cost of sales").Show
End Sub
Sub Display_Original()
'
' Display_Original Macro
' Shows Original scenario
'
' Keyboard Shortcut: Ctrl+Shift+O
'
    ActiveSheet.Scenarios("Original").Show
End Sub
```

Exhibit 7-5: The edited VBA code for the Display_lower_cost_of_sales macro

Review questions

1 What is a macro?

2 List two ways to create a macro.

3 In what type of code, or language, does Excel save macros? Where can you view and edit this code?

4 How do you create a macro that runs when the workbook is opened?

5 What is unique about a function procedure?

6 How do you specify a return value in a function?

Course summary

This summary contains information to help you bring the course to a successful conclusion. Using this information, you will be able to:

A Use the summary text to reinforce what you've learned in class.

B Determine the next courses in this series (if any), as well as any other resources that might help you continue to learn about Excel 2010.

Topic A: Course summary

Use the following summary text to reinforce what you've learned in class.

Unit summaries

Unit 1

In this unit, you used the **logical functions** IF, AND, OR, and NOT to evaluate a condition and return a value based on whether that condition is true or false. You also used **nested functions** to perform complex calculations. Next, you used the **math** and **statistical functions** SUMIF, SUMIFS, COUNTIF, COUNTIFS, AVERAGEIF, and AVERAGEIFS to conditionally summarize, count, and average data. Then, you rounded off a number by using the **ROUND** function.

Unit 2

In this unit, you used the **PMT function** to calculate the periodic payment for a loan. You used **date functions** to calculate the difference between two dates, and **time functions** to determine the number of hours worked. Next, you created an **array formula** that performed multiple calculations on multiple sets to obtain multiple results. You also created an array formula using a SUM function. Finally, you learned how to **display**, print, and hide formulas. You also changed **calculation settings** and iteration limits.

Unit 3

In this unit, you used the **VLOOKUP** and **HLOOKUP** functions to find a specific value in a worksheet. You used the **MATCH** function to find the relative position of a value in a range. You also used the **INDEX** function to find a value in a range by specifying a row number and column number. Finally, you created one-variable and two-variable **data tables** to project values.

Unit 4

In this unit, you created **data validation** rules to control data entered in cells. Then, you used **database functions** to summarize values that meet complex criteria.

Unit 5

In this unit, you learned how to **export data** from Excel to other formats. You also **imported data** from a text file and an XML file. Next, you exported XML data by using the **XML Source pane**. Finally, you used **Microsoft Query** to retrieve data from an Access database, and you used the **Web query** feature to get data from a Web page.

Unit 6

In this unit, you used **Goal Seek** and **Solver** to meet a target output for a formula by adjusting the values in the input cells. Next, you used the **Analysis ToolPak** to create **scenarios** to save various sets of values in a worksheet.

Unit 7

In this unit, you ran a **macro** that automatically performed tasks. You recorded a macro and assigned the macro to a **command button** as well as to a button inserted into the worksheet. You also added a macro button to the Quick Access toolbar and to the Ribbon. Then, you created an **Auto_Open** macro, which runs when the workbook is opened. Next, you **edited** the VBA code for a macro. Finally, you created **custom functions**.

Topic B: Continued learning after class

It is impossible to learn how to use any software effectively in a single day. To get the most out of this class, you should begin working with Excel 2010 to perform real tasks as soon as possible. We also offer resources for continued learning.

Next courses in this series

This is the last course in this series.

Other resources

For more information, visit www.axzopress.com.

Glossary

Array

A collection of rows or columns that is usually defined as a cell address. However, arrays can also be defined as raw data or values, otherwise known as *array constants.*

Array formula

A formula that performs multiple calculations on one or more sets of values, and then returns either a single result or multiple results. You must press Ctrl+Shift+Enter to create an array formula, which is enclosed in braces { }.

Arguments

The values that a function uses for calculations.

Auto_Open macro

The only macro that runs automatically when the workbook it contains is opened.

Circular reference

An error created when a formula refers to the cell containing the formula.

Comments

Non-executable lines of text used to describe sections of macro code.

Cube functions

Functions that are used for data analysis and enable users to retrieve SQL Server Analysis Services and OLAP data directly into cells.

Data table

A range that displays the results of changing certain values in one or more formulas.

Database

An organized collection of related information.

Date functions

Functions used to insert the dates or to calculate length of time in terms of years, months, or days.

Field

A column of data in a database. Also, a category of data in a PivotTable.

Function procedure

A procedure containing the code which, when executed, performs a sequence of steps and then returns a value.

Goal Seek utility

A tool used to solve a formula based on the value that you want the formula to return.

HLOOKUP

A horizontal lookup function used to find values in a table that has column labels.

Input cell

The location where various values are substituted from a data table.

Iteration

The repeated recalculation of worksheet formulas until the maximum number of calculations is reached.

Macro

A series of instructions that are executed automatically with a single command.

Microsoft Query

A program used to retrieve data that meets certain conditions in one or more tables of a database.

Modules

The special sheets in which VBA code is stored.

Nested function

A function that serves as an argument of another function.

ODS (Open Document Spreadsheet)

A file format that maintains some formatting, but not all, when Excel data is exported to it. ODS files can be opened in other spreadsheet applications, such as Google Docs.

OLAP (Online Analytical Processing)

A type of database that stores data to be analyzed. In an OLAP database, the relationships and hierarchies are stored in OLAP cubes, which provide a multi-dimensional way to look at data.

PDF (Portable Document Format)

A file format that preserves formatting and enables file sharing. PDF provides a standard format for use by commercial printers. Adobe Reader is available as a free download.

Quick Style buttons

Buttons located on the Format tab and used to apply several formatting properties at once to a selected graphic.

Record

A row of data in a database.

Return value

The result of a function procedure.

Scenario

A set of input values that produce different results.

Solver utility

A tool used to perform complex what-if analysis by adjusting the values in multiple cells used in a formula.

Sub procedure

A procedure containing the code which, when executed, performs a sequence of steps.

VBA (Visual Basic for Applications)

The code, or language, in which Excel saves the steps of a macro.

Views

Different sets of worksheet display and print settings that you can save.

VLOOKUP

A vertical lookup function used to find values in a table that has row labels.

What-if analysis

The process of changing the values in a worksheet and observing how these changes affect the results of formulas.

XML (Extensible Markup Language)

A set of rules for structuring and designing data formats that are exchanged between applications.

XPS (XML Paper Specification

A file format that preserves formatting and graphics when Excel data is exported to it. XPS Viewer is installed by default.

Index